HOUSE PLANTS
in colour

ROB HERWIG

HOUSE PLANTS
in colour

David & Charles
Newton Abbot London

ISBN 0 7153 7464 8

©1975, 1976 Zomer & Keuning Boeken B.V., Wageningen

This translation ©1977 Zomer & Keuning Boeken B.V., Wageningen

Printed in Holland
for David & Charles (Publishers) Limited
Brunel House Newton Abbot Devon

Frontispiece: *Yucca aloifolia* show to best advantage when displayed on its own

Author's Introduction

This book on house plants contains a selection from the large assortment available and shows in full colour practically all those plants which can be grown successfully. In addition, a number of rarer specimens are mentioned, interesting items that florists occasionally have for sale.

In order to help you check the growing conditions of individual plants, their requirements as regards light, temperature, watering, humidity and soil are summarized at the end of each entry. Plants with similar requirements are listed in the appendix at the end of the book.

The book opens with a chapter on the general care of house plants, It is advisable to begin by reading this section, as it explains many of the terms used in the subsequent text.

To give you an idea of the effects which may be achieved with house plants, there are photographs of a number of interiors in homes and offices where plants are being used in original ways. The advantages and disadvantages of modern plant containers are discussed, and reference is made to indoor office gardens and to hydroculture.

I hope that this book will provide professionals as well as amateurs with all the information they may require. Comments and suggestions for additions are welcome; and I should like to express my grateful thanks to all those who have cooperated in the production of the book.

ROB HERWIG

Contents

A fine example of the vigorous Aloe arborescens *in a plastic cylinder*

The Care of House Plants

House plants will thrive only if you provide the right conditions, and for this a certain amount of basic knowledge is essential. The information in the next few pages can be used as a guide to the brief summaries at the end of the descriptions of each plant in the main section giving details of its main requirements as regards light, temperature, water, humidity and soil.

Light

When considering the amount of light required by various plants, we distinguish between full sun, light shade, shade and deep shade. *Full sun* means that a plant prefers an unscreened south-facing window. *Light shade* may be created in the same window—for instance, by half-closing a venetian blind—but an east-facing window, which receives full sun only until about 10am, may also come under the heading light shade. When we speak of *shade* we might mean a north-facing window not darkened by trees, but the term applies equally to a position about 1–2m from a south-facing window. *Deep shade*, finally, refers to positions which receive very little daylight; for instance, at a distance of several metres from a window. Only the very strongest plants can survive in so little light.

In order to simplify matters I have worked out a system by which the strength of light received may be easily determined. This should be done at noon on a cloudless day in May or July. Use a photographic light meter, or, if necessary, a camera with a built-in light meter (see photograph). Adjust to 50ASA (=18DIN) and read at 1/125 of a second. Hold the measuring cell 20cm away from a piece of white card. The diaphragm figure will give you the strength of the light, as follows:

Full sun: f16–20 (approx. 160–320,000 lux)
Light shade: f8–11 (40–80,000 lux)
Shade: f4–5.6 (10–20,000 lux)
Deep shade: f2.8 (5,000 lux).

5,000 lux at midday, is about the minimum. If you want to place a plant in an even less-favoured position you will probably have to use artificial light: spotlights (es-

pecially low-pressure types) will help to some extent, but two 40-watt 'daylight' fluorescent tubes, placed 60–80cm above the plants, are better.

Time-controlled systems can be built into a double ceiling to illuminate the plants—as shown in the adjacent photograph (the circular openings in the ceiling). Plants require at least 6 hours of 'sleep', i.e. darkness, in every 24 hours. The on- and off-periods are easily controlled with the aid of a time-switch. If you dislike the rather bleak light provided by fluorescent tubes or mercury lamps, you could set the clock to switch on during the night, from 2 or 3am until 8am.

Shading against excessive sunlight is best done by means of aluminium venetian blinds (see photograph), but even a thin net curtain will be of help. Yellowing foliage may be a sign of too much sun.

Temperature

By no means all plants will thrive in a living-room kept at a constant temperature of 20°C (68°F). Rooms with single-glazed windows are fortunately a little cooler, and many plants benefit from this (the *Cyclamen*, for instance). Large plants that prefer cooler conditions are better grown in a hall, corridor, unheated bedroom or somewhere similar. In this book we always indicate the minimum night temperature in summer: 16–20°C (61–68°F) is considered warm, 10–16°C (50–61°F) moderate, 3–10°C (37–50°F) cool. Night temperatures have been chosen because during the day temperatures may vary enormously with the intensity of sunlight. Near a closed window a reading of 40°C (88°F) may easily occur—hardly favourable to plants. Indoor temperatures of over 44°C (95°F) are in fact generally fatal. On the other hand tropical plants will readily tolerate 35°C (79°F), provided the light is adequate.

In winter many plants enjoy a resting period, when their temperature and light—and, consequently, moisture—requirements are lower: many cacti and other succulents must be kept dry at 5–8°C (41–47°F). Where a plant does require a resting period, the minimum winter temperature is indicated.

In modern centrally heated houses it is difficult to create a satisfactory winter environment. It may be possible to keep the garage at 5°C (41°F), and a convenient window or skylight may admit adequate light. Otherwise you might consider an aluminium lean-to greenhouse placed against a wall of the house and kept frost-free by means of thermostatically controlled heating. In summer such a greenhouse may be used to grow tomatoes.

Water

The amount of moisture in the soil in the pot is, if anything, even more important than the correct temperature. Plants in small pots, in particular, easily become either too wet or too dry and, when the sun is shining, it may be necessary to water three of four times a day, especially when the pots are made of clay. Plastic pots do not allow

evaporation and thus maintain to a certain extent the moisture level in the soil.

Frequently too much water is given. This is not serious if the pot has good drainage, has holes and is placed in a saucer, but in ornamental containers, and particularly in the modern plastic plant cylinders, it can be disastrous (see the section on potting, p. 10).

Water requirements in the growing season vary considerably from plant to plant. Where we say keep *dry*, it is sufficient to trickle a few drop of water just inside the rim of the pot from time to time. The soil must remain friable and feel fairly dry. *Moderately moist* means that the soil is allowed to dry out almost entirely before watering again. *Constantly moist* indicates that one should always be able to feel moisture when testing with the finger. *Wet* means that water appears when one presses the soil

with a finger. Of course it is difficult to measure moisture correctly. There are moisture meters on the market and these are very useful, but a sensitive finger does the trick almost as well.

If a plant is kept drier than it should be its leaves curl and eventually drop, while if the soil is too damp, growth is checked, the leaves remain small and the soil is covered in fine green moss.

Most watering cans on the market are both ugly and impractical. A good watering can is not too small (3–5 litres (5–9 pints)), and has a long spout, enabling you to reach plants standing far back. An example is shown in the photograph.

A special method of watering is to *plunge* the pot in water. This is often done in the case of shrubby plants in well-drained pots from which excess water can be shed.

Plunging removes air from the soil as can be seen from the little bubbles that will appear in the water. Leave the plant for about half an hour and then allow it to drain so that the soil absorbs fresh air. A small amount of fertiliser may be added to the bath, which should be kept at 20–30°C (68–86°F).

In the case of sensitive plants

(e.g. azalea, hortensia) soft water should be used. Tapwater is often unsuitable. If the hardness of your water supply exceeds 150ppm (parts per million—your local water department will tell you), it should not be used for acid-loving plants (see plant descriptions). Rainwater is best, provided it has first been brought to the correct temperature. An oily layer on the surface of the water in the butt is a clear indication of pollution, and such water should never be used. The only other solution is to soften the tapwater. Ordinary domestic water softeners, in which kitchen salt is used, are unsuitable for this purpose since they merely exchange the 'hard' calcium and magnesium ions for the sodium ions in the salt. The carbonate hardness, damaging to sensitive plants, is not reduced —in fact, it is slightly increased. So the tapwater should be softened by total or partial demineralisation. The apparatus for this is filled with minute plastic grains which, in effect, trap everything except the H_2O itself. After a time the filling discolours and must be replaced. Distilled water can be bought from chemists and garages, but it is cheaper to use your own apparatus.

If you need only small amounts of softened water, use melted ice cubes from the refrigerator.

Humidity

Atmospheric humidity, which affects the extent to which a plant transpires (loses water to the atmosphere), is something quite separate from the moisture needed at a plant's roots, and this important condition is therefore indicated separately in the plant descriptions. Cacti and other succulents generally tolerate a dry atmosphere; on the other hand, plants originating in rain forests, such as orchids, many ferns and thin-leaved foliage plants, require a high degree of humidity.

Transpiration depends on a plant's number of pores per unit area of its surface, their size, and also whether the plant is able to close its pores. Specimens with shiny, leathery leaves, such as many *Ficus* varieties, transpire only slowly and are therefore tolerant of dry air. Most succulents are even more adaptable, since they can close their pores entirely.

Centrally heated houses are, as a rule, very dry, since little fresh air enters from outside—and the same is true of a room with a fire. Forced ventilation solves the problem; hot-air heating may, in fact, be ideal for many plants as it can provide complete air conditioning.

Frequent spraying, preferably with lime-free water to avoid a

white deposit on the foliage, may increase the atmospheric humidity to some extent. Water containers hung on radiators are not very satisfactory since they dry out very quickly. Where a small plant is concerned, place the pot above a deep plate or a bowl filled with water in such a way that the foliage is moistened by evaporation.

By far the best solution is to purchase an electric evaporator or humidifier. In a humidifier the water is expelled in minute particles by means of an electric motor. It is not noise-free and, unless lime-free water is used, furniture, windows, etc., will in the

course of time be covered in a white deposit. An evaporator is the modern equivalent of a kettle boiling on the hob; however, the water does not actually boil, but is thermostatically maintained at a temperature of 95°C (203°F). This apparatus is noiseless; current consumption is approximately 300watt and about 400cc (about $\frac{3}{4}$ of a pint) of water evaporates every hour. Lime is retained in the water and may be removed from time to time with a descaler. I have been using the type of evaporator shown in the photograph for several years and find the system very satisfactory.

Soil

A standard, proprietary potting compost is suitable for many, but not all, plants. Some plants like acid soil, rich in humus, and this is indicated in the plant descriptions in the main body of this book. You can compose such soil yourself by mixing standard potting compost with peat fibre (preferably coarse fragments), beechleaf compost or pieces of rotted wood—a sackful of suitable material can quickly be collected in any forest. Other plants may prefer chalky, porous soil: in this case the standard potting compost should be mixed with coarse sand, shards of crockery, pulverised clay or loam, perlite, etc. Potting compost based on domestic refuse may also be used.

Special mixtures are available for cacti and for *Anthurium*; it should also be used for bromeliads. A special mixture, containing chopped fern roots as well as

sphagnum moss, is used for orchids; it is usually obtainable from orchid growers.

If you decide to make your own mixture, it is best to do so a few months before use—although this is not essential. The photograph shows (clockwise, starting top left): peat fibre, coarse sand, pre-packed potting compost, sphagnum moss.

Potting and re-potting

The illustration shows a small selection from the large assortment of flowerpots now available. At

one time all house plants were grown in red clay pots, thought to be best because of their porosity, but we now know that roots can absorb the necessary air *via* the surface, provided it is kept friable. A great deal of water is evaporated from clay pots, making the soil inside 1–2°C (2–4°F) cooler. In sunshine the moisture evaporates quickly and after a time the pot begins to look unsightly because of the lime deposit. Only those plants that enjoy dry soil from time to time should be grown in clay pots.

On its initial introduction the plastic pot gave rise to difficulties for many growers, because too much water was given. As no water evaporates through the pot wall, a medium-sized plant needs only about $\frac{1}{3}$ of the water it would require in a clay pot.

Ornamental pots are usually lethal because water collects at the bottom, but there are now some acceptable shapes with drainage hole and matching saucer on the market.

Plastic plant cylinders and ceramic pots are non-porous and have no drainage holes. If one wishes to grow plants in these attractive containers it is essential to water with the greatest care: water soon collects in the bottom of the container, and this is extremely harmful to the roots. The water level can be kept down by inserting a length of plastic tubing whose lower end rests several centimetres from the bottom on a good layer of pebbles.

Re-potting is necessary when the root system fills the pot, when the pot breaks, when the soil has become acid, when the plant shows symptoms of disease and, in the case of young plants, at least once a year at the beginning of the growing season. Roots which have grown through the drainage hole should not be cut off; it is better to break the pot. Provided you leave the soil-ball intact, re-potting can take place at any time of the year. If a section of the root system is damaged in the process, it is advisable—if possible—to remove part of the foliage as well.

The new pot should be a few sizes larger with drainage provided by one or more crocks (see photograph). Put a thin layer of fresh soil in the bottom and place the soil-ball on top after removing a little of its upper layers. Surround the soil-ball with fresh soil, pressing down well, and finish with a 2cm (1in) top layer of fresh soil. Make sure that room is left for watering.

Feeding

Even if a plant is given fresh, nutritious soil every year, it may need feeding after a few months. The more rapidly a plant grows, the more nutrient it needs. As a rule this is administered in the shape of a chemical fertiliser (either in liquid or in powder form), but organic fertiliser, such as dried cow manure, dried blood, horn- or bone-meal is equally suitable. It is important never to exceed the quantities indicated; it is better to give repeated doses of a weak solu-

tion than infrequent doses of a strong solution. It is also advisable to alternate different products.

During the dormant season, when the plant develops few, if any, leaves or flowers, feeding is unnecessary. At such times the nutrient would not be absorbed and this might lead to excessive and harmful mineral concentration.

In many cases better results are achieved by repeated re-potting than by endless feeding. The pot-soil eventually turns into a kind of rubbish-bin for everything the plant is unable to digest and in such an environment the roots will perish. A good rule to follow is: the more you have to water and feed, the more often should a plant be re-potted. Note our comments about clay *versus* plastic pots.

Taking cuttings

Growing new specimens from cuttings is one of the most rewarding jobs in the care of house plants. Many species root easily and will produce new plants within a few months. In some cases it is essential repeatedly to grow new plants from cuttings, as the old plant becomes unsightly. Cuttings will often root in water, but better results are achieved in a mixture of equal parts of coarse sand and fine peat. On the windowsill the rooting mixture will remain fairly

cool, and not all plants will root at this temperature; woody plants certainly will not. Leaves left on the cuttings must not be allowed to let too much moisture evaporate, for there are as yet no roots to make up for the loss. Many plants will therefore root more easily in a plastic indoor propagator heated electrically. A thermostat is unnecessary. The photograph shows such a propagator.

Cuttings may be taken in various ways. The best known method is to take tip-shoots, about 6–8cm ($2\frac{1}{2}$–3in) in length, cut just *below* a leaf joint. The lower leaves are gently removed and the cutting is inserted in the growing medium. An eye cutting, for instance of a *Ficus*, consists of a section of stem with one leaf; the leaf is rolled up in order to reduce evaporation.

The new plant will grow from an almost invisible eye in the axil.

The leaves of foliage begonias, *Sanseviera* and other plants may be cut into sections from which roots will develop. In the case of other species, such as for instance *Dracaena*, the cuttings may consist of sections of the stem.

A very special method of propagation is air-layering. Here the cutting is induced to form roots before it is severed from the mother plant. This is done particu-

larly in the case of *Ficus, Monstera, Philodendron, Syngonium,* etc. A leaf is removed from a node, an incision is made in the stem, a match inserted in the cut and the whole thing is wrapped in damp sphagnum and plastic (see photograph). Roots will develop within a few weeks.

Sowing

As a rule seeds are sown in early spring when the light improves. The seedbed may consist of a proprietary potting compost thinned with an equal amount of coarse sand. Special seed compost is also available. Use a small indoor propagator (see photograph), which need not necessarily be heated. Many seeds require extra heat in order to germinate, and in such cases the propagator illustrated on p. 11 is better.

First, two seed leaves appear, followed by a pair of true leaves.

Now the seedlings must be pricked out—i.e. given more room to develop (see photograph). For this purpose you should use fresh potting compost, still somewhat thinned with sand. Keep the propagator closed for some time.

Bottle gardens

There was a period when it was fashionable to grow plants in bottles. Although this is now less often done, a well planted bottle remains an attractive sight. Because of the high degree of humidity, conditions are almost ideal for the plants. The moisture transpired from the leaves condenses on the glass during the night and flows back into the soil, to be reabsorbed by the roots. Where the moisture content is perfectly balanced, all condensation will disappear in the course of the

morning.

Use a clear or pale coloured demijohn with either a narrow or a wide neck (photograph). The bottle should first be thoroughly cleaned with hydrochloric acid and water. A layer of nutritious soil is then inserted *via* a funnel, made by rolling up a newspaper. The plants are put in position by means of a fork and a spoon tied to wooden rods: manipulate these tools until the plants are where you want them. Use graceful foliage plants, such as *Fittonia* and *Episcia*, which do not grow too large.

After planting, a stopper is inserted to make the bottle airtight. The contents form a little world of their own and a little water need be added only after several months.

Pruning

Pruning may become necessary for one of several reasons.

1. Immediately after re-potting larger specimens. The more the root system has suffered, the more foliage should be removed. A correct balance between roots and foliage encourages growth.

2. When a plant grows too large, some of its branches may be removed. This should not be done in the case of plants with beautiful stems (*Dracaena*, *Yucca*).

3. Before or after the winter resting period (e.g. *Hibiscus*), in order to maintain a compact and easily handled shape. If possible, pruning should be delayed until growth has ceased.

4. In order to delay flowering, for instance in the case of *Fuchsia*. Budding tips are removed to encourage side shoots, which will produce further buds.

Pruning should always be done *above* a leaf joint or eye. An eye will develop into a new shoot; its position will dictate the direction of the shoot, especially in shrubby plants. Avoid crossing branches; keep the shape open so that all shoots will receive adequate light. If the plant bleeds after pruning, the wound should be staunched with charcoal or ash.

Hydroculture

Plants may be grown in water just as well as in earth, and the system is called hydroculture. In the smaller hydropots which have been on the market for some time, the plant is set in a container filled with pebbles. Part of the root system grows between the pebbles, thus absorbing air; the larger part hangs down in the water in the pot. As a rule glass pots are green, to minimise the growth of algae.

Another idea now popular, particularly for large arrangements and in office gardens, is to fill

large containers with clay granules, with a nutrient solution at the bottom. The water level is checked by means of a water-gauge or a floater. From time to time the water is replaced by a fresh solution. Special care is taken to maintain the correct pH (the acidity of the water). The use of these hydro-containers therefore requires some knowledge of the subject.

The greatest advantage of hydroculture is that to a large extent the plants are cared for automatically—of special importance in offices. In private homes the system might be useful if the inhabitants are often absent, for a hydro-container may be left unattended for weeks on end. However, to my mind it remains preferable to grow plants in soil. (See also p. 21.)

Holidays

When you go on holiday, soil-grown plants require special measures. If you are unable to find a friend or neighbour who is will-

ing to look after them, you should resort to technical aids. The photograph shows a kind of mushroom made of porous clay; this is filled with water and closed with a plastic cap. The porous shaft is placed in the soil; capillary action allows water through only when the pot-soil has reached a certain degree of dryness. As the shaft is connected to a water supply by means of plastic tubing, the water level in the mushroom remains constant. This system will suffice for months on end, provided the water supply is adequate. You would do well to try it out first.

In another method, porous threads are drawn through the pot; the ends hang in a bowl of water. Here it is essential to use very large bowls, as otherwise the water supply would be used up within a few days. Yet another, less successful, system is to place all the plants together in a bath, in which they rest on porous bricks. Sometimes people wrap large plants in plastic sheeting—this is frequently an invitation to all kinds of disease.

If you possess a garden the hardier plants might be planted in damp peat.

Diseases

Innumerable products are sprayed onto house plants by the credulous; it is the manufacturers who benefit most. Are they any use? True, the pests will be killed, but as a rule they return in full force within a few weeks, since spraying has not removed the *cause* of the disease. What is worse, these products—often of a very dubious nature—may be poisonous to people and to pets.

Plant diseases are frequently caused by lack of nutrition; that is, the plants have not been re-potted in good time or they have been fed incorrectly. It is also possible that the acid content of the soil has risen as a result of hard water. Another cause may be that the plant is kept in an unfavourable situation—too cold, too warm in winter, etc. You can check this with the plant descriptions in this book.

If the plant is badly affected, it should be drastically pruned, well rinsed in warm water and re-potted in fresh soil. For subsequent care follow the instructions given in this book. Ten to one the plant will recover.

If spraying is unavoidable, choose harmless products based on pyrethrum and/or derris. The label should indicate the contents so the choice presents no problem.

Effects to be Achieved with House Plants

The time when house plants were displayed only in a row of pots on the windowsill appears to be behind us. Of course a reasonably wide windowsill remains an excellent place for plants, particularly when attractive pots are used. However, there are many other ways in which plants may play a part in interior decoration. Just look at the man-sized *Yucca gloriosa*, practically a tree, illustrated on the facing page. Other ideas for growing plants away from the windowsill will be found in the following pages.

When interest in interior decoration began to grow, attention was also given to house plants—and their ugly pots. It is difficult to date the beginning of this conscious interest, but it became very obvious once the plastic plant cylinders came on the market. The underlying principle was that the entire plant, including the container, should be regarded as a decorative element (to this one should add: make sure that it will flourish in the position you give it—for this is sometimes forgotten). Existing pots did not fit into modern interiors, and in the search

for something different the plastic plant cylinders were developed. Originally they were made of drainage tubes, sprayed in modern colours. These are still the most attractive, but because they are somewhat pricey (they are largely made by hand) there was soon a demand for cheaper versions, which are now available. Plant cylinders are available in all sizes, from very low and wide to very tall and narrow. This has the advantage that the container can be chosen to fit the depth and width of the plant's root system, for some plants have a long taproot while others have a wide, shallow root system.

At about the same time the so-called Sintoform containers came on the market. These are round, oval, square or hexagonal polyester containers, usually white, with a wide, slightly inward-curving upper edge. An example can be seen on p. 17. Smaller, narrower cylinders in many beautiful colours were made in ceramics (see p. 16, the *Cyperus*).

It was also at about the same time that it became fashionable to grow plants in glass tanks, of which an example is shown on

Facing: Yucca gloriosa in a plastic cylinder
Left: Three specimens of Dracaena fragrans, here in the form of Ti-trees of varying heights, together in a plastic cylinder

This vigorous Aspidistra elatior has been growing in its tall red cylinder for two years

p. 18. Attractive effects may be achieved by alternating layers of soil and sand. To show you how a rather dull plant, such as an *Aspidistra*, may be turned into a show piece, I have photographed a specimen in a tall red cylinder placed in a modern white interior. The *Aspidistra* is one of the strongest plants for a warm room and it is satisfied with so little light that it will do well as much as 4 to 5m from a window, as in the photograph. It is unfortunately rarely seen these days.

Not only in the living-room

As I said on the preceding page, house plants need not be confined to the windowsill or, indeed, to the living-room. The photograph below shows a good-sized modern bedroom where the green foliage of the Umbrella palm (*Cyperus alternifolius*) harmonizes well with the deep yellow floor covering. The plant's position near the window is, moreover, satisfactory and, provided the soil is kept moist, the *Cyperus* will flourish for many years. House plants may also be grown successfully in bathrooms and kitchens, where the atmosphere is generally damp. Needless to say, there should be adequate light; a bathroom with a tiny window is suitable only for some African violets or other small plants on the windowsill.

A well-lit room which is rarely used will provide an ideal winter environment for succulents and other plants which like to be kept cool in the dark season.

Not all plants will enjoy a long life in the living-room. Some, such as bromeliads, die after flowering; others have too great a need for humid air to survive in the long run. There are also plants which are attractive only while they are in flower; this applies, for instance, to many begonias. One may decide to buy a plant even though one knows in advance that its ornamental value will be only temporary. The beautiful fern *Nephrolepis exaltata*, above right, will certainly be a fine sight for at least 2 to 3 months, particularly if it is sprayed daily. It is a magnificent plant, particularly placed in this tall white pot. When it becomes bare it may

Nephrolepis exaltata, *here temporarily used for ornament*

easily be brought back to life in a greenhouse. Do not forget that ferns like to be generously fed.

And what about all those wonderful bromeliads, such as *Aechmea, Ananas, Neoregelia* and *Vriesea*? Every flowering rosette will die—in fact it is already dying. It is therefore of little importance if the plant is placed in a dark spot or in too dry an atmosphere. In fact, the flower will last a little longer if kept fairly cool. All in all these are ideal plants for problem corners, where nothing else will grow.

In summer many plants prefer to live on the balcony or in the garden. The *Camellia* and the *Azalea* should be put in the shade, but the *Yucca*, the *Hibiscus*, the *Agave* and the *Agapanthus* like bright sunshine. The different requirements are easily checked. The minimum night temperature indicated will tell you whether an outdoor position may be too cold. The word used for such plants is 'cool', but it does not matter if during the day the temperature should occasionally rise to 35°C (95°F).

House plants should always be well protected against wind, particularly on a balcony.

A beautiful Cyperus alternifolius *brightens up a bedroom*

The flower window

The flower window—which was, I believe, invented in Germany—is a kind of indoor greenhouse. It usually takes up the space of an entire large outside window and may be built out, or into, the room.

Flower windows may be open on the inner side, but a tropical window is separated from the room by a glass partition, such as you see in the photograph. Within the enclosed space the climate may be regulated as desired by means of electric heating, thermostats, humidifiers, automatic screening and artificial lighting. For a clever handiman or a wealthy grower the possibilities are practically limitless. Needless to say plants will flourish in such ideal conditions.

Indoor trees

This is my name for the enormous plants which are becoming so fashionable. They are extremely decorative—the photograph of the 2m-tall *Dieffenbachia amoena* will prove it. It is placed in a polyester Sintoform container. Other plants may grow equally tall; large specimens of *Ficus benjamina*, palms, *Yucca* (see p. 14) and many others are obtainable. If they have been properly hardened there is no reason why they should not do well in the living-room, provided, of course, that both temperature and light are correct. Imported plants are sometimes disappointing. As a large indoor plant is very expensive, you should first check whether you have a suitable place for it.

It is not generally known that cheaper plants such as *Abutilon* or *Sparmannia* may grow into very tall trees within a short time. My own variegated *Abutilon* grew to 6m (20ft) within two years.

Plants in the office

In recent years the use of house plants in offices has increased enormously. No doubt this is due to the fact that modern offices are often so lacking in atmosphere that only plants can make them tolerable. Whatever the reason, the trade benefits, for large sums are involved and floral decorators are kept very busy. The technical jargon interspersed with Latin names used by these specialists sounds impressive to the layman, but in my opinion there are not all that many firms who are really knowledgeable, so be careful whom you employ. Make sure that the plants you get will thrive in the positions allocated to them. A dark hall with two fluorescent tubes at a height of 3m (10ft) is emphatically *not* the right place, but the number of expensive arrangements I have seen in such positions are legion. It is, moreover, very important that in heated offices (usually kept at 20°C (68°F) only plants that enjoy a warm environment are used.

If you must have a plant at some

This Dracaena deremensis *'Warneckii' receives some fluorescent light as well as indirect daylight*

distance from a window, make sure it is brought nearer the light after office hours. This applies, among others, to the fine *Araucaria* in the glass container shown in the large photograph. On the desk it receives a certain amount of fluorescent light, but this is not enough. Closer to the window, where a *Dracaena* is growing in a yellow cylinder, conditions are acceptable.

The large *Dracaena* in the smaller photograph stands at a distance of 4m (13ft) from a large, west-facing window and therefore receives a certain amount of evening sun. This appears to be adequate, for the plant has stood in this position for more than two years and seems to be flourishing.

To my mind it is also very important that the floral decorator's ideas should fit in with those of the interior designer, for otherwise the general effect will be a mess.

In this book I have purposely illustrated modern interiors, which may guide you in planning your future environment. Fortunately employers and employees are becoming more and more discriminating and rightly make high demands for their environment.

The Araucaria *shown here receives too little light in this position, and should be occasionally placed near to the window*

Office landscapes

There is now great interest in office landscapes and office gardens. Large areas are sound-proofed and are then divided merely by screens, differences in floor level, and especially by plant containers. This creates semi-open spaces for desks and rest areas. The photograph below shows such an office garden in which the area has been divided by a plant trough. Since as a rule little daylight reaches the centre of these office landscapes, extra lighting must be installed. In this case fluorescent tubes have been introduced above the plants, while a number of spotlights create special effects.

It cannot be said that this is entirely adequate. It would have been better if three rows of fluorescent tubes had been installed—or, even better, a set of high-pressure mercury lamps. The plants would have developed more foliage and would last longer.

In practice we frequently find plants being used in positions which receive little daylight and which thus become lanky and unsightly. For large firms, in particular, the additional cost of installing artificial lighting is relatively small in relation to the total investment in office greenery.

Something to think about . . . ?

Section of an office landscape with artificial lighting

The choice of plants for offices

As a rule containers installed in offices are filled with a mixed assortment of plants. I am rather against this, not only because the combinations are frequently very ugly but more particularly because it is difficult to combine plants with corresponding growing requirements. One plant prefers a little more light, another likes drier soil, for a third the average pot-soil is too acid, a fourth is obviously suffering from too high a temperature. The usual result is that some of the plants perish while others thrive, and the combined effect which had been planned is ruined.

Above: Dracaena marginata
Below right: Pandanus veitchii
Below left: Monstera deliciosa

It is therefore advisable wherever possible to use individual plants in reasonably sized, preferably mobile, containers. It is always possible to combine a number of containers in order to achieve an attractive combination. If the bare soil under a large plant is disliked, a suitable groundcover may be found; that is, a modest-growing plant which does not compete with the main plant. Small-leaved ivies are suitable for this purpose, but do not like too warm an environment, in which *Ficus pumila* or *Ficus radicans* would be better. Various forms of *Cryptanthus* or *Pellaea* are also suitable.

Some varieties of *Dracaena* (an attractive motherplant is seen in the photograph) are particularly strong. Motherplants have been used by the grower for taking cuttings and as a result are widely branched. The large *Pandanus* is a unique example; it appears to feel very much at home in this well-lit office. The large photograph shows a Swiss cheese plant with enormous leaves—a truly magnificent specimen.

Other very suitable plants are: *Abutilon* (rarely seen), *Aloe arborescens* (p. 6), *Aspidistra*, *Cissus*, *Cyperus*, *Dieffenbachia*, *Ficus benjamina* and *Ficus lyrata*, *Howea*, *Microcoelum*, *Pellaea*, *Philodendron*, *Phoenix*, *Rhaphidophora*, *Rhoicissus* and *Scindapsus*.

Hydroculture

As it appears to be very difficult to give house plants exactly the right amounts of water and food (I cannot understand why, but it remains a fact), research was undertaken into other methods. As we have seen, hydroculture had long been known. Most plants will thrive if they develop aerial roots as well as water roots. Personally I have never found that they grow *better* in hydroculture than in soil, but many people insist that this is so. Plants for hydroculture must be specially grown—or at any rate they have to get used to this method of growing. This is done in specialised nurseries.

One popular system is to grow the plants in closed containers partially filled with a nutrient solution. The plants themselves remain in their original plastic containers. Eventually the roots (which in this method remain much smaller) grow through the openings. The remaining space in the outer container is filled with clay granules, which provide support and air. The level of the nutrient solution is checked by means of a gauge. The water is replenished weekly and twice a year the nutrient solution is replaced. The correct degree of acidity is important: it should lie between pH 5.7 and 6.8.

In another system the bottom of the containers is covered with a

layer of clay granules, on which a mat made of a porous manmade substance is placed, followed by a layer of soil. Water and food is transported to the roots *via* the mat. Here, too, the nutrient solution must be regularly replenished and renewed. As a rule ordinary tapwater is unsuitable for the preparation and replenishment of the nutrient solution, because it contains too many minerals and is too hard. Rainwater, or the use of a demineralising apparatus, is therefore essential in this case. If a lime-free fertiliser is used it is advisable to add 20% tapwater to supply calcium.

It is interesting to study the morphological differences between soil- and water-roots. Soil-roots

Plants in combination in special hydrocontainers under the Luwasa system

An example of an indoor garden using expanded clay granules

are vigorous, thick and well-branched. They have short, thick extremities (the root-hairs). In hydroculture the root system is much less vigorous, whereas very long, fine root-hairs are developed. When plants with soil-roots are transferred to hydroculture, the soil-roots die first; water-roots develop soon afterwards.

In many cases the choice of system will depend on maintenance opportunities. Often hydroculture will prove to be cheaper, but we have as yet too little practical experience to be certain that this is always the case. I would advise a firm's management to have a look at both hydroculture and soil systems which have been established *for at least 2 years.*

Abutilon

The *Abutilon* is a shrubby plant from the tropics; it is a source of amazement to many people who see it in my house, for I grow 5m (16ft) specimens within the course of about two years. This is by no means a difficult feat, for the *Abutilon* is extremely vigorous. The only thing to bear in mind if you wish to achieve similar results is that the plant should be re-potted in good time. Starting in early spring with a cutting, the young plant can be put in a 12cm (4½in) pot within at most two months; in late May it should be transferred to a 20cm (8in) pot and by early August you will need a small tub. During the winter the plant can remain in this, for in September growth will gradually cease. In winter a cool situation is preferable (approx. 10–15°C (50–59°F)) but, if you don't mind the leaves dropping, it can stay in the living-room. Re-pot in March into a larger tub and within two months you may have to consider a tub with a diameter of 60–80cm (2–3ft). By late July the tallest shoots may have reached 5m (16ft). Naturally such a plant requires plenty of water: about 10 litres (about 18 pints; 10 US quarts) on a sunny day. Support is essential, for the long shoots are limp. In the third year the plant will become too large and you should grow a new one.

If you do not re-pot in time, the *Abutilon* will almost certainly be attacked by mealy bug.

The large specimens described above are achieved primarily with the beautifully marked *Abutilon striatum* 'Thompsonii' (lower photograph, left foreground). This is in any case the finest variety; it has orange flowers. Green-leaved *Abutilon* hybrids, with red or yellow flowers, may be grown from seed.

The upper photograph shows *Abutilon megapotamicum*, nicknamed 'Belgian flag' because of the colours of its flowers; these are of an entirely different shape. A green-leaved variety exists as well as a variegated form.

☼ Full sun essential for flowering

🌡 Moderate (10–16°C (50–61°F) at night); minimum temperature in winter 12°C (54°F)

💧 Plenty of water in summer; water moderately in winter

〰 Reasonably tolerant of dry atmosphere in winter

🪣 Slightly chalky potting compost

Acacia

Mimosa

Although the plant usually sold as a *Mimosa* is a different variety, the *Acacia armata* illustrated bears a close resemblance to it. The care of this mimosa is extremely simple, but a cool situation in winter is absolutely essential. In summer the pots, which should not be too large, are best placed in a sheltered, sunny outdoor position. The variety illustrated does not grow beyond 80–150cm (30–60in); a true *Mimosa* would soon outgrow a greenhouse. Propagation is best achieved from cuttings with a 'heel'. Seed has to be prepared, as it does not easily germinate.

☼ Always a well-lit position

🌡 Cold (3–10°C (37–50°F) at night); cool situation in winter essential

💧 Water moderately; soil must not dry out

No special requirement

Normal to slightly chalky soil, possibly with the addition of some sand

Acalypha

These fine plants originate in the Australian archipelago. They are particularly attractive in appearance: one species has long red tails and the other produces beautiful variegated foliage. That they are used as house plants is undoubtedly due entirely to their appearance, for since they require a high degree of humidity their cultivation presents problems. As a rule it proves impossible to keep the *Acalypha* through the winter.

If, nevertheless, you want to have these fine plants on a permanent basis, you will in most cases have to resort to cuttings, and this is none too easy. If you decide to try, spring is the only possible time. Adequate bottom heat is essential.

The photograph shows *Acalypha hispida*, the red-hot cat's tail or chenille plant. The tails may grow as long as 50cm (20in). As a rule they are red, but there is a white form called 'Alba'. Dead flowers should be removed.

The other photograph shows a detail of the

24

Acalypha (continued)

chenille plant's sister species, *Acalypha wilkesiana*. Here the flowers are far less conspicuous, but the leaves are much more beautiful. 'Musaica' shows a mozaic pattern in red and orange; 'Marginata' has orange-brown, pink-edged leaves; in 'Obovata' the foliage is olive-green with an orange margin, eventually fading; and 'Godseffiana' develops spotted leaves with a creamy margin.

In my experience these plants may be kept indoors provided they are regularly sprayed. In a greenhouse they present no problems. Watch out for red spider.

☀ Plenty of light necessary for fine colouring; direct sun is harmful

🌡 Moderately warm (10–16°C (50–61°F) at night), minimum of 17°C (50–63°F) in winter

💧 Keep moderately moist

༄ Requires a high to very high degree of humidity throughout the year

⊍ Normal to loamy soil

Achimenes

This plant is grown from scaly root-stock kept dry in winter. In summer, purple and pink forms of *Achimenes* hybrids are usually sold in flower, but other varieties are obtainable which you can bring into growth yourself in damp peat fibre, at fairly high temperature and humidity. An indoor propagator is practically indispensable for this purpose. During the flowering period, the plant should be generously watered and fed. Towards the autumn it is gradually allowed to die back by withholding water. The dead stems are removed and throughout the winter the rhizomes (root-stock) are kept in dry peat fibre at the minimum temperature indicated below.

☀ A fair amount of light, but out of direct sunlight

🌡 Warm (16–20°C (61–68°F) at night); minimum of 14°C (57°F) in winter

💧 Water moderately

༄ Likes a humid atmosphere

⊍ Requires acid, porous soil, e.g. *Anthurium* mixture

Acorus

Sweet-flag

The ordinary sweet-flag is a waterplant used in garden ponds. The *Acorus gramineus*, or grass-like sweet-flag in the photograph is a native of Japan and is not winter-hardy. Indoors it has approximately the same requirements as the well-known Umbrella plant (see *Cyperus*); that is, the soil should be kept constantly moist. You would do best to put the pot in a large saucer filled with water. The most beautiful form is the variegated 'Variegatus' illustrated. Propagation is by division of existing plants. Provided the temperature is kept moderate, the care of these plants presents no problems.

☼ Tolerates a fair amount of shade, but a position near a net-curtained south-facing window is acceptable

🌡 Cold to moderate (5–10°C (41–50°F) at night), to 25°C (77°F) by day in adequate ventilation

💧 Water frequently; does not mind a footbath

💦 Normal room atmosphere provides adequate humidity

🪣 Somewhat loamy potting compost

Adiantum

Maidenhair fern

The maidenhair fern is now rarely found in the living-room, as it does not tolerate dry air. The plants are best given a resting period in winter; the old foliage is removed. During the growing season plenty of water and, particularly, regular feeding are desirable.

In the photograph you see (left foreground) *Adiantum tenerum*. The leaf-stems are deep black; there is great variety in the shape and colour of the foliage. *Adiantum cuneatum* (right) is much more freely branching. Here too, numerous forms exist for use indoors. It is particularly useful as groundcover.

☼ Prefers a shady situation

🌡 Warm (16–20°C (61–68°F) at night), minimum 16°C (61°F) in winter

💧 Water often with tepid water; plunge if necessary. The soil-ball must on no account dry out

💦 Does not tolerate dry air; likes regular spraying

🪣 Special fern mixture or acid potting compost

Aechmea

Aechmea is a member of the large Bromelia family, a group of plants with leaves growing in rosettes, usually with a fine inflorescence. All bromeliads have in common that the rosettes die after flowering. They are therefore 'disposable' plants which may be placed in any position, for while they are flowering the foliage is already dying.

During flowering one or more baby rosettes develop at the foot of the plant. As soon as the old foliage is obviously deteriorating (this may take a fairly long time), the young rosettes may be removed and grown separately. Growing instructions are given below. With luck the new plants will flower in a year or two. In the growing season in particular it is advisable to pour some water into the funnel from time to time. If the plant is growing well, but does not flower, try wrapping it in a plastic bag for a few days, together with some ripe apples. The gas released by the apples induces flowering.

By far the best known species is *Aechmea fasciata*, illustrated above; it has green and white marbled foliage. The inflorescence consists of pink bracts and small blue flowers which later fade into pink. The entire rosette may grow to a diameter of 60cm (24in). The lower photograph shows *Aechmea fulgens*, another popular species, with dark green leaves. Here the inflorescence consists of oblong racemes of coral-red calyces, from which blue, berrylike flowers appear.

Less well known species are *Aechmea chantinii*, with conspicuous horizontally striped leaves and small red flowers in yellow bracts; *Aechmea miniata* with narrow green leaves and a red raceme in which only the small petals are blue; and finally *Aechmea weilbachii*, which has green rosettes of narrow leaves, while the raceme is coral-red with blue sepals.

☼   Likes a well-lit position; tolerates diffused sunlight

🌡   Warm (16–20°C (61–68°F) at night)

💧   Keep the pot-soil moderately moist

  Preferably fairly humid, but will tolerate a dry atmosphere

  A porous mixture, including, for instance, woodland soil, sphagnum moss and peat fibre, or bromeliad compost

Aeonium

These plants develop particularly fine rosettes, unusually placed at the top of succulent stems. This is because the lower leaves are continually dropped, creating the effect of a Bonsai tree. When detached, rosettes root fairly easily.

The species illustrated is *Aeonium balsamiferum*. A form more frequently encountered is *Aeonium arboreum*, which grows wild along the Mediterranean. *Aeonium domesticum* is a low-growing species. In summer the plants prefer to stand out of doors; the pot should be buried in the soil. In winter treat as succulents. Re-pot in spring, but only if necessary.

☼ A very well-lit position is excellent; only the midday sun should be avoided

🌡 Moderate (10–16°C (50–61°F) at night)

💧 Requires little water; the pot-soil should dry out in between watering. Use clay pots rather than plastic

〰 Likes a dry atmosphere

🪴 Somewhat chalky mixture

Aeschynanthus

These plants greatly resemble the *Columnea* (q.v.), which at one time was cultivated on a larger scale; however, it appears that *Aeschynanthus* is now gaining in popularity, which is undoubtedly due to its rich flowering and its striking inflorescence. Nevertheless we should never forget that, like *Columnea*, *Aeschynanthus* needs a humid atmosphere, so that the dry air of a living-room will certainly create problems. Frequent spraying helps to some extent, but the use of a humidifier is even better (for people also).

On this page you see the species *Aeschynanthus lobbianus*. The good thing about this plant is that the empty dark-coloured calyces in the foreground will later produce flowers; these start as small round balls at the bottom of the calyces. If you buy this plant covered in calyces you can be sure that it will flower for several months, provided you maintain a sufficiently high temperature.

A different species, *Aeschynanthus pulcher*, has drooping stems and brilliant red flowers in summer.

Aeschynanthus (continued)

A third fine species is *Aeschynanthus speciosus* (upper photograph). The small-flowered species with marbled foliage, *Aeschynanthus marmoratus*, is now rarely grown.

In the care of these plants it should not be forgotten that they were originally epiphytes from damp forests. The pot-soil should therefore preferably be mixed with sphagnum. If the plants are grown in hanging pots do not forget to water in good time. In winter they may be kept cooler and drier; this will encourage flowering. Propagation is from cuttings, which will strike only under glass or plastic and in extra bottom heat.

☼   Slight shade is best

🌡   Warm (16–20°C (61–68°F) at night); during the resting period 18–20°C (64–68°F); to encourage bud formation a little lower (12–15°C (54–59°F))

◊   Water moderately with tepid water

〰   A high degree of humidity is desirable

▬   Normal to humic soil mixture

Agapanthus

This member of the Lily family, a native of Africa, can be grown indoors but feels happier on a sunny balcony or in the garden. A constant succession of the beautiful flowers will appear from July to September. In winter the plant should be given a cool but frost-free situation, for instance in a slightly heated garage kept at about 5°C (41°F). In spring the fleshy roots are gently re-potted, but this need not be done every year. They are in fact easy and graceful plants to grow. Good species are *Agapanthus africanus* and *Agapanthus praecox*. The strongest forms are the hybrids; these can remain out of doors in winter if covered with straw.

☼   Requires plenty of sunshine

🌡   Moderate (10–16°C (50–61°F) at night); the cooler the plant is kept in winter (provided it is frost-free), the better it will flower

◊   Keep moderately, but constantly, moist

〰   Normal living-room atmosphere is sufficiently humid

▬   Somewhat loamy garden soil

Agave

No doubt you know that there are many *Agave* species. The larger forms are found growing wild in all southern countries, while further north they are frequently grown in tubs. As it may take as much as sixty years for an *Agave* to flower, species with interesting foliage are most in demand. The most popular one is the so-called Century plant, *Agave Americana*. The upper photograph shows the variegated form 'Marginata'. In 'Medio-picta' and 'Striata' the stripe runs down the centre of the leaf instead of along the margin. If the plant *should* every produce a flower—at the top of a metre-high stem—its end is approaching.

The smaller species are more suitable for the windowsill. They develop beautiful rosettes of variously coloured leaves. The lower photograph shows *Agave filifera*, which develops thin hairs along its leaves. *Agave ferox* has much wider, vigorous, fleshy leaves ending in sharp points; they are a beautiful steel blue in colour.

Another exceptionally fine form is the fairly small *Agave victoriae reginae*. This plant develops a very regularly shaped, spherical rosette, consisting of dull green leaves 10–15cm (4–6in) long with a narrow white margin.

Many other species will be found in the catalogues of cactus and succulent growers.

All species may be stood out of doors from late May onwards, but this is not essential. A cool and very dry situation in winter is highly desirable.

When re-potting, a good layer of crocks should be placed in the bottom of the pot and the soil should be mixed with 30% of coarse sand. This is the best way to guarantee adequate drainage.

Agaves are easily grown from seed. It is also possible to take the runners, where these are developed, and plant them in sandy soil after letting them dry out.

☼ If possible in full sun; they may be put outside in summer

🌡 Moderate (10–16°C (50–61°F) at night); minimuum in winter 4–6°C (39–43°F)

◊ Requires little water

〰 Insensitive to dry air

▼ Requires chalky potting compost

Ageratum

In some countries the *Ageratum* is best known as a garden or balcony plant, but it can be grown indoors as well; in the United States this is often done. Young plants are bought in spring, planted in normal potting compost and placed near a sunny window, preferably in a well-ventilated situation. It is possible to keep them through the winter, to be grown into large plants in the following season. In spring, cuttings may be taken; these are best grown in an indoor propagator. Plants may also be raised from seed, sown in heated soil from February onwards.

 A sunny position

 Moderate (10–16°C (50–61°F) at night)

 Soil must be kept constantly moist; water moderately

 Likes a moderately humid atmosphere

 Preferably somewhat loamy garden compost, or else a proprietary potting compost

Aglaonema

Chinese evergreen

Few people know the name of this plant, which resembles the *Dieffenbachia*—to which it is related. They are actually hothouse plants, but a number of species can be grown in the living-room, especially in combination with other plants. One of the best known forms is the hybrid 'Silver Queen' illustrated. *Aglaonema costatum* is of spreading habit; it has dark green white-blotched leaves. The plants do best in wide shallow pots filled with friable soil. They can be propagated from tip cuttings set in a heated indoor propagator.

 Tolerates a great deal of shade as well as diffused sunlight

 Warm (16–20°C (61–68°F) at night); in winter the temperature may fall to 14–18°C (57–64°F)

 Water generously during the growing period, using tepid water; keep somewhat drier in winter

 Moderate humidity

 Slightly chalky soil, rich in humus

Allamanda

Allamanda is a tropical climber which will thrive only in a high degree of humidity. It is best grown in a heated greenhouse. Nevertheless there are people who, by means of frequent spraying, succeed in keeping the plant in good condition and even in bringing it through the winter. A humidifier in the house is of course a great advantage. Tie the long shoots to wires or up a wall; cut them back drastically in winter in order to restrict evaporation. Propagation is from cuttings grown in heated soil. The photograph shows *Allamanda cathartica*.

 Light to medium shade

 Warm (16–20°C (61–68°F) at night)

 Water moderately during the dormant season; generously in the growing period

 High degree of humidity essential; it can be kept in the living-room only if frequently syringed

Somewhat loamy soil

Alocasia

Magnificent foliage plants from tropical Asia, related to *Anthurium*, these should be cared for approximately as is *Caladium* (q.v.). This means a great deal of moisture, in the atmosphere as well as in the soil, and a fairly high temperature; they should be kept moderately dry in winter though should not be allowed to dry out as much as *Caladium*. Naturally a heated greenhouse is the best solution, but the plants can be kept for some months in the living-room—especially *Alocasia sanderiana*. A plant case or a flower window would of course be excellent for the purpose. Propagation is from shoots or from division of the root-stock. Sowing is also possible.

 Slight shade preferred

 Warm (18–20°C (64–68°F at night); in winter, too, the temperature should not fall below 18°C (64°F)

 Soil should be kept fairly moist

 Humid atmosphere: syringe regularly

Friable, slightly acid mixture, for instance leaf-mould, peat fibre and sphagnum

Aloe

This genus of succulents embraces a large number of species, on the whole easy to grow. It should not be confused with the *Agave*, which belongs to the Amaryllis family; the Aloe is a member of the Lily family. It flowers much more easily than the *Agave*.

In the photograph I have assembled a few well-known species, of which two are in flower. Above right is *Aloe variegata*, undoubtedly one of the forms most suitable for the windowsill. Its leaves are beautifully marked. Above left is a small specimen of *Aloe arborescens*, the tree-shaped aloe, which may grow to as much as 3m (10ft). New side shoots are constantly produced. This species, too, flowers readily. Below right is *Aloe humilis*, which remains small and has a prickly leaf rosette. The small plants below left are called *Aloe bakeri* and *Aloe stans* (syn. *Aloe nobilis*). These are less well known, but give an indication of the habit and ability to flower of the smaller species.

It is not all that difficult to keep an *Aloe* in good condition for many years, particularly if you keep the pots well drained and make the soil mixture extra porous by the addition of coarse sand and perlite. Stagnant water is fatal, especially at lower temperatures. You should also avoid spilling water on the foliage, for this will remain in the hollows at the base of the leaves and cause decay.

If you want the plant to flower it is better to keep it at about 8°C (46°F) in winter, practically ceasing to water. On sunny days in summer extra generous watering is fully justified. Liquid fertiliser is also useful. The plant can be increased by rooting side shoots, but can be grown from seed, which germinates readily: this is the simplest method to obtain rare species.

 Full sun if possible

 Moderate (10–16°C (50–61°F) at night); keep cool in winter

 Water moderately in summer, hardly at all in winter

 Very tolerant of dry atmosphere

 Somewhat loamy potting compost; ensure adequate drainage

Ampelopsis

You really should try this *Ampelopsis brevipe-dunculata* var. *maximowiczii* 'Elegans', if only because of its imposing botanical name! It is as easy to grow as its name is difficult to pronounce, provided you place the plant out of doors from time to time and keep it cool, especially in winter. In the cold season most of the foliage will probably drop, but after re-potting in spring (I advise you to do this every year), new leaves will soon appear. The plant feels most at home in a cool hall. If you have a patio it can be planted outside; it will survive the winter if given light protection. Propagation is from cuttings.

☼ Semi-shade

🌡 Moderate (10–16°C (50–61°F) at night) to cool (3–10°C (37–50°F)); requires a cool situation in winter

💧 Water moderately

💨 Fairly tolerant of dry living-room atmosphere

🪣 Calcareous mixture

Ananas

Pineapple

This ornamental form of the edible pineapple produces small fruits topped by a shock of leaves. This is clearly shown in the photograph of *Ananas comosus* 'Variegatus'. The plants are fairly expensive, but they are incredibly strong and even in a shady room will give you pleasure for at least six months. As in all bromeliads the old rosette will then die, but the good thing about this plant is that it is easy to grow a new one from the shock of leaves at the top of the fruit. which should be cut off together with a thin slice of the flesh. Leave to dry for a few days and then plant it in sandy soil or even in pure sand, moderately warm: you will soon have a new plant.

☼ Plenty of light and sun

🌡 Warm (16–20°C (61–68°F) at night); temperature in winter 15–18°C (59–64°F)

💧 Keep the soil fairly moist; more water in the growing period

💨 Fairly high degree of humidity required

🪣 Standard potting compost

Anthurium

Flamingo plant

Since World War II the flamingo plant has become very popular, as a house plant as well as for cutting. The flowers keep well in water.

Anthurium is a tropical plant, requiring warmth and humidity, but the modern *Anthurium scherzerianum* hybrids (above left in the photograph) are reasonably tolerant of the dry atmosphere in a living-room, particularly when they have been hardening off for some time in the florist's shop—provided always that the shop was not too cold, for low temperatures can do irreparable damage. The best known colour is scarlet, but pink, blotched and even white forms are sometimes available.

Anthurium andreanum hybrids are the forms usually grown for cutting, but they may serve as house plants as well (on the right in the photograph). Spray the leaves frequently with tepid water and never water with tapwater: this is far too hard. See the introduction on the subject of water softening.

The third species illustrated is *Anthurium crystallinum* (foreground), which derives its decorative value chiefly from the fine foliage. In this case living-room air is definitely too dry; this species can be successfully grown only in a greenhouse. It is essential to re-pot *Anthurium* every year, mainly to get rid of the very harmful unabsorbed minerals retained in the old soil. For this purpose you should use special *Anthurium* compost containing sphagnum. Water generously when the plant is in flower, and feed preferably with diluted cow manure.

When re-potting, the plant can be increased by division of larger specimens. When a flamingo plant has become unsightly, the stem may be cut up and the sections rooted in a heated indoor propagator.

 Well-lit position, out of the sun

Warm (16–20°C (61–68°F) at night); minimum of 16°C (61°F) in winter

During the flowering period water liberally, using tepid, lime-free water

Fairly high degree of humidity

Special *Anthurium* compost

Aphelandra

Aphelandra squarrosa was seen far more in the 'sixties than it is today, probably due to the fact that it is difficult to grow in a dry living-room. If you have hot-air heating or possess a humidifier you will probably be more successful.

After flowering, the plant should be kept somewhat drier and cooler. It can be kept through the winter; in the second year it may develop into a good-sized plant. Pruning will encourage new shoots. All this is best done in a warm greenhouse. Propagation from young shoots will succeed only in an indoor propagator.

 Well-lit position out of the sun

 Warm (16–20°C (61–68°F) at night)

 Water freely, especially in the flowering season; the soil-ball must never dry out

 Fairly high degree of humidity; syringe frequently. A little drier in winter

Nutritious potting compost, rich in humus

Aporocactus

Rat's tail cactus

This is one of those old-fashioned hobby plants rarely for sale in a shop. Fortunately it will strike readily and you might be able to obtain a cutting from a friend. Cuttings should be allowed to dry out for a few days before being set in very sandy soil, later to be transferred to a cactus mixture.

The plant is best grown in a hanging pot. In summer it should be watered freely, but in winter it must be kept much drier, as well as cooler, in order to flower.

The species illustrated is *Aporocactus flagelliformis*. In a less well-known species, *Aporocactus flagriformis*, the stems are ribbed.

 Very light and sunny situation

Moderate (10–16°C (50–61°F) at night); keep cool in winter to encourage flowering

 Water freely in the growing season, far less in winter, but do not allow to dry out completely

 Normal living-room atmosphere is sufficiently humid

Special cactus mixture

Araucaria

Araucaria makes a very good specimen plant in all kinds of interiors. Overwatering in the dormant season, inadequate humidity, direct sun or drying of the soil-ball are only a few of the mistakes which may cause loss of the lower branches. Often this creates a decorative effect, but if you dislike a bare stem you might resort to the purchase of one or two more *Araucarias* of varying heights, and plant them all together in a tub. Propagation—amateurs are rarely successful—is from tip cuttings. The photograph shows *Araucaria heterophylla*.

 Fairly good light, but out of the sun

 Moderate (10–16°C (50–61°F) at night); minimum temperature in winter 3–5°C (37–41°F)

 Keep moderately moist, using tepid water

Moderate to high degree of humidity
Acid potting compost, rich in humus and possibly incorporating some sand

Ardisia

Spear flower

The *Ardisia crenata* illustrated is gaining in popularity; deservedly so, for the graceful red berries keep for a long time. If you wish to keep the plant through the winter, it should definitely not be placed in too warm a situation and it should be regularly sprayed. In the following summer the plant will flower for the second time; to encourage fruit formation the pollen may be rubbed in with a little brush.

Ripe berries may be sown in December, but this should preferably be done in a greenhouse. Do not confuse the plant with *Skimmia japonica* (p. 167).

 Well-lit to sunny situation, well-ventilated in the flowering period

 Moderately warm (10–16°C (50–61°F) at night); 12–15°C (54–59°F) in winter

 Keep the soil fairly moist

 Moderate humidity, spray regularly with tepid water; keep drier during flowering

Normal to chalky potting compost

Asparagus

Asparagus fern

If you've ever seen edible asparagus growing you'll be struck by the resemblance. The ornamental asparagus is a strong plant and will even survive ill-treatment. Nevertheless it is now rarely grown.

At one time a great deal of *Asparagus setaceus*—better known by its former name *Asparagus plumosus* (upper photograph, right)—was used in formal flower sprays. It is not exactly a fascinating house plant, but it will keep very well, especially in a dark position. Larger plants will in due course develop tendrils.

Asparagus densiflorus 'Sprengeri', usually called *Asparagus* 'Sprengeri', is an attractive house plant. This, too, is a very strong plant; it will thrive at a distance of several metres from the window. It is illustrated on the left in the upper photograph. Its chief characteristics are small white flowers, a pendulous habit, which makes it suitable as a hanging plant, and prickly tendrils.

An attractive wide-leaved asparagus is *Asparagus falcatus* (upper photograph, centre). It is very useful in plant combinations.

The lower photograph shows a very old-fasioned ornamental asparagus, namely *Asparagus asparagoides*, among older florists probably better known as *Medeola*. In the 'twenties and 'thirties mature tendrils were frequently used as table decoration, to make wreaths for the hair, and so on, for the leaves keep fresh and green for a long time. It is a good hanging plant for the living-room.

All ornamental asparagus plants should be fed almost weekly in summer. They should be re-potted every spring; a good-sized crock should be placed over the hole in the pot to prevent the roots growing through.

The plants are best increased by division, but can also be grown from seed.

☼ Will thrive in well-lit as well as in dark positions

🌡 Moderate (10–16°C (50–61°F) at night) summer and winter

💧 Water frequently in summer, a little less in winter. From time to time plunge the entire pot in water

🍃 Moderate humidity

🪴 Somewhat chalky potting compost

Aspidistra

Although perhaps considered old-fashioned (grandma also grew it), an *Aspidistra* grown in a beautiful plastic cylinder is a fine sight. It is, moreover, exceptionally strong and will thrive well away from a window. It tolerates the dry atmosphere of a living-room even where the temperature is very high, but avoid stagnant water in the pot as well as direct sun. The species illustrated is *Aspidistra eliator*. There is a variegated form 'Variegata', but this is a less hardy plant. Increase by division; this must be done very gently.

 Shady position preferred

 Moderate to cool (8–13°C (46–55°F) at night)

 Maintain a constant degree of moisture

 Moderately high; dry air is tolerated reasonably well

 Chalky potting compost

Asplenium

Spleenwort

The best known species is *Asplenium nidus* or Bird's nest fern shown in the photograph (background). The fronds may grow to as much as a metre in length, but are usually shorter. In the wild this fern grow on trees. Dry living-room atmosphere is tolerated reasonably well, especially if the foliage is sprayed from time to time. Feed generously; keep the soil friable. In the foreground you see the less well-known *Asplenium daucifolium* (syn. *Asplenium viviparum*) which greatly resembles *Pteris tremula* (p. 153). This Asplenium species develops small plantlets on its fronds; these may be removed and grown separately. The Bird's nest fern is grown from spores.

 Requires little light

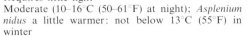 Moderate (10–16°C (50–61°F) at night); *Asplenium nidus* a little warmer: not below 13°C (55°F) in winter

 Requires damp soil which must never dry out. Plunge in water from time to time; water frequently in the growing season

 Fairly high degree of humidity; spray often

 Mixture of loam, leafmould and sand

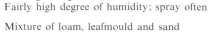

Astrophytum

This genus embraces particularly fine cacti, regularly available at the florist's. The photograph shows a flowering *Astrophytum myriostigma* or Bishop's cap. The body of the plant is covered in innumerable small white flakes. The other species illustrated is *Astrophytum ornatum* or Star cactus, with spiralled ribbing also covered in white spots. There is also *Astrophytum asterias*, the Sea urchin, consisting of a flat sphere; this species has woolly white areoles instead of spines.

All species must be kept cool in winter, otherwise they will not flower. Progagation is from seed.

☼ Well-lit, sunny situation (semi-shade for strains without spines)

🌡 Warm (16–20°C (61–68°F) at night); cool (5–10°C) (41–50°F)) in winter

💧 Sparingly in summer, none in winter

💨 Very low humidity

🪴 Special cactus mixture or loamy soil

Aucuba

This is an excellent plant for a holiday house which remains unheated in winter. Provided it is watered from time to time, it will stand up to frost, for the common *Aucuba japonica* 'Variegata' grows wild in temperate coastal zones. In the warmth and dry atmosphere of a heated living-room the plant will have a hard time in winter. A cool hall, a garage or an unheated room are suitable places. The yellow-spotted ornamental form 'Crotonifolia' will tolerate a slightly higher temperature. Increase from cuttings in moderate bottom heat; it can also be grown from seed, but this takes time.

☼ Satisfied with little light

🌡 Cold (3–10°C (37–50°F) at night); ornamental strains must be kept frost-free in winter

💧 Keep moderately moist in summer; water sparingly in winter

💨 Fairly tolerant of dry atmosphere; syringe occasionally in winter

🪴 Garden soil rich in humus

Azalea

The correct names of indoor azaleas are *Rhododendron indicum* (upper photograph) and *Rhododendrum obtusum* (below), but most plant lovers still call them by their old name *Azalea*, so that is where they are placed in this book. *Rhododendrum obtusum* also grows in gardens, where it is known as the Japanese azalea. The greatest attraction of growing azaleas is, of course, to induce them to flower in subsequent years. After flowering in early spring the plant should be placed in a frost-free position, but as cool as possible. It will develop a number of new shoots, but these must be removed after a few weeks. Shoots appearing after mid-April may be left, for towards the end of May the *Azalea* should be placed in the garden or on the balcony, where it will continue to grow. A shady, not too dark spot is best.

If the pot is small, the plant should first be re-potted in acid soil, preferably soil from below fir trees, or garden peat mixed with cow manure. It is best to use plastic pots to prevent the soil-ball from drying out. Give a little extra fertiliser in July. Azaleas may also be planted without pots in prepared soil. By late September buds will have formed and the plant may be brought indoors.

Do not immediately place it in a warm living-room, where it would drop its buds: it may be brought into a heated room only when flowering starts and should then be placed as close to the window as possible, as it will be slightly cooler there. Spray as often as possible.

Japanese azaleas may be treated in the same way, but they may also remain in the garden, where they should be given some protection in their first winter.

Always water azaleas with rainwater or softened tapwater and occasionally plunge the pots in a bath. Propagation from cuttings is difficult for amateurs, as this requires a green-house.

☼   Well-lit position, but does not tolerate full sun

🌡   Moderate to cool (5–15°C (41–59°F) at night)

💧   Water liberally in the flowering season, preferably by plunging in tepid water

   Moderate humidity; in a dry room the plant should be syringed once a day

   Acid soil

Begonia

Begonias are among the most widely grown and diversified house plants—hence no fewer than three pages are devoted to them in this book. Nearly all species are extremely easy to propagate, especially from tip or nodal cuttings. Your hand need only, it seems, touch a good shoot and you have a new plant growing in your living-room!

On this page, to begin with, are two species which can also be grown in the garden or on the balcony. If you want to grow them indoors, a first requirement is to keep them cool; this applies particularly to the tuberous begonias. If you can keep them below 20°C (68°F) in summer they will hardly know where to stop. The upper photograph shows a *Begonia semperflorens* hybrid. These plants are often grown from seed, especially for use as bedding plants. The so-called F_1 hybrids are the most vigorous, though not necessarily the most beautiful. The most common colours are white, pink and red and there are single as well as double forms. The foliage is green or bronze-coloured. After one or two years the plants clearly deteriorate. If you possess a good strain it is easy to take cuttings; these will root even in water.

In the lower photograph you see a number of large-flowered tuberous begonias. Actually the small-flowered and hanging forms are the finer. In winter the tubers are kept dry at 10°C (50°F); from mid-March onwards they are brought into growth in damp peat in a moderate temperature; they are then potted. Tubers with more than one shoot may be divided.

After the growing season, either indoors or out of doors, water should be gradually withheld until finally, at about the end of September, the stems are cut off and the tubers lifted. Leave them to dry before storing them in dry peat fibre.

Moderate daylight; diffused sunlight if necessary, but never full sun

Cultivate in a cool situation (5–15°C (41–59°F) at night); minimum of 10°C (50°F) in winter

Keep constantly moist

Any atmosphere is acceptable in the flowering season

Proprietary potting compost with the addition of some peat fibre

Begonia (continued)

An important commercial group consists of the so-called winter-flowering begonias. It is true that other begonias may flower in winter as well, and that winter-flowering forms may also flower in other seasons; nevertheless this particular group is called winter-flowering because at one time it was an unusual quality that these hybrids (for that is what they are) flowered in winter.

The small-flowered type is known as the Lorraine begonia (upper photograph). It occurs in numerous colours and has a very prolonged flowering season. The plants require a fortnightly feed and a great deal of light. After flowering the stems should be shortened and the plants must be allowed to rest. They are then re-potted before being brought into growth once more.

The large-flowered winter-flowering begonias are called Eliator hybrids. They occur in the same colours as tuberous begonias, but the flowers are often single, though occasionally double or semi-double. These plants are even more sensitive to the notorious mildew disease than the small-flowered forms.

This sensitivity explains the success of the Rieger begonias (the lower photograph shows 'Schwabenland'), a vigorous strain with medium-sized flowers. These are not so easily attacked by mildew as the large-flowered strains. Other colours are now on the market as well.

To encourage begonias to flower in winter it suffices to switch on a 60watt bulb, placed 50–80cm (20–30in) above the plant, at dusk. Leave the light on till bedtime. This artificial prolongation of the day will induce flowering throughout most of the winter. Experts grow these begonias from seed, but where small quantities are concerned it is easier to grow cuttings. Both side shoots and tip cuttings are suitable for this purpose.

☼ Plenty of light, but not in full sun

🌡 Normal room temperature or a few degrees lower;
the latter will improve the keeping quality

💧 Keep constantly moist

〰 Ensure moderate humidity

🪴 Proprietary potting compost with the addition of
a little extra peat

Begonia (continued)

Among the many species of foliage begonias the *Begonia rex* hybrids (upper photograph) are the best known. The leaves have a metallic sheen and occur in the most magnificent colours. In a fairly cool, not too dry environment, for instance in a factory, an entrance hall or a moderately heated room (15–18°C (59–64°F)), these plants can be kept in good condition throughout the winter, even at some distance from a window. Propagation is extremely simple: a leaf is cut into 0.5cm ($\frac{1}{5}$in) square sections and these are pressed on to the growing medium. This must, however, be done in a heated indoor propagator.

Of the numerous botanical begonias occasionally available, a tall shrubby example is shown in the lower photograph. It is easily grown from cuttings and is equally simple in care; provided it is generously fed and re-potted in good time such a shrub may grow to a height of 2m (6ft).

None of the begonias enjoy a long life: after thriving for several months to a year they suddenly deteriorate and are frequently attacked by mildew. If you immediately take a cutting (with begonias this may be done at any time of the year) it will still have a chance to grow into a healthy plant and so the cycle begins again. This is the best way to grow these plants. They should not be compared with, for instance, a *Ficus*, which might be kept for 30 years.

It is best to use plastic pots for begonias. This prevent the soil-ball drying out—something they all detest. On the other hand you must be careful not to drown the plants—they are, after all, not waterplants. Provide adequate drainage and use porous but nutritious compost (mix with leafmould).

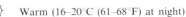

Warm (16–20°C (61–68°F) at night)

Requires a fair amount of light, possibly diffused sunlight, but never full sun

Keep moderately, but constantly, moist, using soft water (pH 4.5–5)

Fairly high degree of humidity preferred

Pre-packed potting compost with peat or leafmould added

Beloperone

Shrimp plant

Though no longer cultivated on such a large scale, the *Beloperone guttata* illustrated is still regularly available at any good florist's. It has a most attractive inflorescence, the fine brown bracts forming the most conspicuous part.

The shrimp plant is among the very few house plants which need not be protected from the midday sun. In summer it may be put on the balcony or in the garden. After the dormant season the plant should be pruned a little, re-potted and brought into growth again. Cuttings can be taken throughout the year.

 A sunny situation

 Moderate (10–16°C (50–61°F) at night); in winter keep at 12–16°C (54–61°F)

 After it starts into growth until August water freely; then reduce watering, but make sure the soil-ball does not dry out

 Fairly tolerant of dry living-room air

 Slightly chalky potting compost

Bertolonia

Though these are exceptionally fine plants for the hothouse, *Bertolonias* cannot be equally recommended for the living-room. Nevertheless they are regularly marketed—hence their inclusion here. The most successful method of growing the plant indoors is in a container in combination with other plants; these will provide some degree of humidity. In a closed plant window or plant case there is, of course, no problem.

Propagate from seed in an indoor propagator in January or February. Young plants are the finest and it is therefore advisable to sow new specimens every year.

The species illustrated is *Bertolonia marmorata*.

 Grows best in a shady spot

 Warm (16–20°C (61–68°F) at night); try to maintain a fairly constant temperature (in summer during the daytime 20–22°C (68–70°F))

 Water moderately freely

 Humid atmosphere essential

 Coarse moorland or pine-forest soil mixed with peat fibre

Billbergia

In the descriptions of most of the bromeliads in this book you will read that young plants are not easily cared for. The opposite applies to the *Billbergia × windii* illustrated here. Even while the main rosette is in flower so many new shoots develop that within a short time you have a complete bunch; the following year several of the rosettes may flower simultaneously. If we consider, moreover, that the plant will do well in almost any position, we may conclude that this is a practically ideal bromeliad, which ought to be cultivated much more. Increase by division of over-large plants.

☼ A well-lit spot preferred, but will accept a fair amount of shade

🌡 Moderate (10–16°C (50–61°F) at night); during the day the temperature must on no account fall below 12°C (54°F)

💧 Freely in summer, sparingly in winter depending on the room temperature

💨 Reasonably tolerant of dry air

🪴 Compost-based mixture or standard pre-packed potting compost

Blechnum

The *Blechnum gibbum* fern (see illustration) is rarely seen; nevertheless it is one of the finest indoor species. Its ideal environment is in a moderately warm greenhouse, where the fronds may reach a length of 1m (3ft). After some years the plant develops a small trunk; it then resembles a palm in habit.

Ensure constant humidity and do not allow the temperature to rise too much. The soil-ball should always be kept moist; feed adequately during the growing season. Propagation is from spores in a heated seed-bed.

☼ Well-ventilated situation; give it plenty of room

🌡 Warm (16–20°C (61–68°F) at night); maximum temperature in winter 16–18°C (61–66°F)

💧 Water very freely from March to July, then moderately. The soil-ball must not dry out

💨 Moderately high degree of humidity. The plant should not be syringed

🪴 Somewhat chalky potting compost, rich in humus

Bougainvillea

The sight of these plants creates nostalgia for the southern countries where enormous *Bougainvillea spectabilis* specimens froth over walls and balconies. The form usually found at the florist's is the *Bougainvillea × buttiana* illustrated, a less vigorously branching strain. It is difficult to bring the plant into flower for a second time; to do this a dormant period at a low temperature is essential in winter. From March onwards it must be given a well-lit, warm position; in late May it is best placed out of doors. If pruning is required this should be done immediately after flowering. Increase in spring from cuttings, in high bottom temperature.

☼   Well-lit and sunny situation

🌡   Warm (16–20°C (61–68°F) at night); 6–8° (43–46°F) in winter

💧   Soil-ball must never dry out. Water freely in summer, sparingly in winter

    Moderate humidity; spray frequently, especially in winter, to prevent the leaves dropping

    Standard potting compost or refuse-based compost

Browallia

Browallia speciosa (illustrated) is a little-known annual house plant marketed from June onwards. It may give you a lot of pleasure until the end of the flowering period, especially if you give it a position where the temperature will never rise to excess. Feed regularly. In February these plants may be sown in a heated indoor propagator. Prick out a few to each pot, pinch out the tips, re-pot them when they are growing well and allow them to harden. All this is much more easily achieved in a heated greenhouse. New plants may also be grown from cuttings, but this is rarely done.

☼   Intolerant of direct sunlight, but likes a very well-lit spot

🌡   Moderate (10–16°C (50–61°F) at night); not very sensitive to temperature

💧   Keep the soil-ball moderately damp

    Reasonably tolerant of dry atmosphere

    A somewhat chalky soil mixture rich in humus, or normal potting compost

47

Brunfelsia

The full name of the plant in the photograph is *Brunfelsia pauciflora* var. *calycina* (syn. *Brunfelsia calycina*, *Franciscea calycina*). While some people think it is difficult to grow others find it easy. Important factors are a moderate but constant temperature and attention to the two dormant seasons. The first of these falls in winter: temperature 12–14°C (54–57°F), little water. The second occurs after flowering—that is, about May–June—when the plant should again be kept fairly dry. It may be placed out of doors, provided it is not in the sun. Propagation from cuttings will be successful only in a heated tray, in which the plants may also be grown from seed.

☼ Semi-shade, definitely no direct sunlight

🌡 Moderate (10–16°C (50–61°F) at night); very sensitive to fluctuating temperatures

◊ Water moderately, a little less in the dormant seasons

⸚ Requires a fairly high degree of humidity

🪴 Normal or slightly calcareous mixture

Caladium

This tuberous plant is now rarely grown, but greenhouse owners (increasing in number every year!) could gain a lot of pleasure from it. It is potted in March and brought into growth (in the greenhouse) at about 25°C (77°F) and in a high degree of humidity. Once the leaves are growing well the plant may be gradually hardened. It may keep for months, even in a cool living-room or hall. From the end of September onwards gradually decrease the water supply until all the foliage has died. The tuber may spend the winter either in or out of the pot. The variety illustrated is *Caladium bicolor* 'Candidum'.

☼ Somewhat shady position

🌡 Warm (16–20°C (61–68°F) at night)

◊ Water freely in spring and summer, then gradually decrease

⸚ Fairly high degree of humidity, but do not syringe the foliage

🪴 Mix equal parts of leafmould and peat fibre, adding a little sand

Calathea

The three best known of the approximately one hundred and fifty *Calathea* species are illustrated. *Calathea ornata* (above) has striped leaves, the stripes turning ivory in more mature plants. In the centre is *Calathea makoyana*, sometimes called the Peacock plant because of the feathery design of the olive-green stripes and ovals on a paler green background. The lancet-shaped leaves of *Calathea lancifolia* (below left) are regularly marked with alternate large and small dark green blotches. In many of these plants the undersides of the leaves are in various shades of red.

Calathea does best in shallow pots; deep pots can be partly filled with crocks. The best soil to use is a humusy, coarse and porous mixture, easily made up from leafmould, soil from under conifers, peat fibre, sphagnum and a little charcoal. Good drainage is essential.

Here too, the high degree of humidity required creates a problem. Daily spraying with tepid water helps a little, but it is not enough. The pot may also be placed above a bowl filled with water to create a damp environment; the pot must remain dry. A more expensive solution is the purchase of an evaporator. As the soil is exhausted fairly rapidly, it is advisable to re-pot once a year in June or July. For the same reason the plant should be fed every fortnight.

Late June is also the best time for propagation. This may be done in two ways: by division or from tip cuttings. To encourage rooting, the temperature is best kept at about 17°C (63°F). Like the pot-soil, the growing medium must definitely be friable and porous.

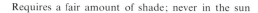

☼ Requires a fair amount of shade; never in the sun

🌡 Warm (16–20°C (61–68°F) at night); not below 16–18°C (61–66°F) in winter

◊ Water moderately, using tepid, soft water. The soil-ball must not dry out

  High degree of humidity, especially when the leaves appear

  Potting compost with the addition of polystyrene granules; or, better still, a special mixture

Calceolaria

Slipper flower

The *Calceolaria* hybrid most generally available is *Calceolaria × herbeohybrida* 'Multiflora Nana'. Because of its attractive colouring and unusually shaped flowers it is a most popular house plant.

Nevertheless it is somewhat demanding. It should never be put in too warm an environment or in a draught, for this will be a direct invitation to aphids. In addition it requires a slightly humid atmosphere, the soil must not be too damp and it must be kept out of the sun. If all these demands are met the plant will give pleasure for a long time, but it must be regarded as an annual. Propagation is from seed in July–August.

☀ A well-lit position, out of the sun

🌡 Cold (3–10°C (37–50°F) at night)

💧 Reasonably moist soil; water regularly and do not let the soil-ball dry out

💨 Fairly high degree of humidity required

🪣 Potting compost rich in humus

Callistemon

Bottle brush

Callistemon citrinus (formerly called *Callistemon lanceolatus*) is one of the few species whose unusual inflorescence occurs at an early stage in its development. The red colour is provided by the stamens. It is rather surprising that *Callistemon* is so rarely grown in the living-room, for it is easy to care for.

It is best re-potted in early March. For successful flowering it requires fresh air and light. Prune drastically in spring, to encourage a bushy habit; afterwards give a lime-free feed every fortnight until August.

☀ Well-lit situation; preferably place out of doors in summer

🌡 Moderate (10–16°C (50–61°F) at night); keep cool in winter (6–8°C (43–48°F))

💧 Water moderately, using soft water

💨 Tolerates dry air

🪣 Potting soil mixed with peat fibre; the soil must be lime-free

Camellia

This is a very conservative plant; it dislikes change, such as temperature variations, irregular watering or being moved. Even a change in humidity frequently causes it to drop its buds. Until the buds open, the plant should be kept at a maximum temperature of 12°C (44°F); it may then be kept a little warmer. After flowering keep at about 6–10°C (43–50°F), and from May onwards outside.

The photograph shows *Camellia japonica* 'Chandleri Elegans'; this is the strongest variety.

Propagation is from tip cuttings in January–February. Use a hormone rooting powder.

☼ Light shade; in summer in the garden or on the balcony

🌡 Cold (5–10°C (41–50°F) at night); the plant is sensitive to temperature variations

💧 Water fairly freely, using tepid water

〰 Average humidity

🥛 Acid mixture (pH 4.5–5.5); it must be friable, porous and rich in humus

Campanula

Bell flower; Star of Bethlehem

An old-fashioned house plant, but still very popular. The varieties most generally available are the white *Campanula isophylla* 'Alba' and the blue 'Mayi'.

Its cultivation is relatively simple. In sunny weather water frequently to avoid yellowing of the leaves. In winter place in a cool room, after removing the foliage. Water very sparingly, more freely in spring when the plant starts into growth, when it should be fed as well. Insufficiently rich soil leads to yellowing foliage.

Taking cuttings is child's play: use 5–10cm (2–4in) long tip shoots.

☼ Well-lit spot, keep out of the sun

🌡 Cool to moderate (5–12°C (41–54°F) at night); very sensitive to frost

💧 Maintain constant moisture; soil-ball must on no account dry out

〰 Moderate humidity

🥛 Somewhat calcareous mixture, rich in humus

Canna

Originally *Canna* was a garden plant, growing fairly tall especially in southern regions, and consequently unsuitable for use indoors. Dwarf forms of *Canna indica* have now been developed, such as 'Lucifer' (left in the photograph). 'Perkeo' is all red; 'Puck' is yellow. They are fine ornaments for your windowsill; an added advantage is the fact that they need not be screened even from the brightest sun. However, the large surface area of the foliage means that a great deal of moisture is evaporated in these circumstances, so that generous watering is essential. Propagation (from offsets of the root-stock) is a job for a knowledgeable amateur.

☼ Requires plenty of light and sun

🌡 Warm (16–20°C (61–68°F) at night); keep in a moderately warm room in winter

◊ Water moderately; liberally in hot weather

🌬 Tolerant of normal room conditions; enjoys fresh air from time to time

🪣 Proprietary potting compost; feed weekly. In spring re-pot in fresh soil

Capsicum

Red pepper; Chillies

The plant is usually sold with the fruit already formed and ready to ripen; it is therefore in the last stage of its one-year life. If you want to see the *Capsicum annuum* in all its phases, you must sow it yourself, under glass, in February–March. Be sure to maintain an adequate temperature. After a month the little plants may be pricked out and gradually hardened. A sunny position, a temperature of about 15°C (59°F) and moderately moist soil will ensure early flowering. To ripen the fruits plenty of sunshine is required.

☼ If possible a sunny spot, but preferably no sun between 10am and 5pm

🌡 Moderate (10–16°C (50–61°F) at night); in summer the plants may be placed out of doors

◊ Requires fairly moist soil; water regularly

🌬 Reasonably tolerant of dry air

🪣 Somewhat chalky soil mixture

Carex

Sedge

Among the *Carex* species only *Carex brunnea* is suitable for use as a house plant. The form 'Variegata' illustrated has a white margin to the leaves. This evergreen plant is particularly useful for introducing variety into a plant arrangement.

Its care presents practically no problem, except that the soil-ball should not be allowed to dry out.

Propagation is usually by division, for sowing produces all-green plants.

☼   Good light, but avoid direct sun

🌡   Moderate (10–16°C (50–61°F at night); 8–16°C (46–61°F) in winter

💧   The soil-ball must remain moist; water moderately

🗎   Moderate humidity

🥛   Chalky potting compost rich in humus

Catharanthus

The *Catharanthus* genus occurs wild from Java to Brazil. Of the five species only *Catharanthus roseus*, a native of Madagascar, is suitable for use as a house plant. The oval leaves have central white veins. The 'Alba' variety illustrated produces red-centred white flowers. Another species has rose-red flowers. If you study the photograph carefully, you will no doubt be struck by the plant's resemblance to the well-known garden plant *Vinca minor* (periwinkle). It is for that reason that the *Catharanthus* was formerly called *Vinca rosea*. This shrubby plant is usually grown from seed as an annual, but it may also be grown successfully from cuttings.

☼   Requires a well-lit, sunny position

🌡   Moderate (10–16°C (50–61°F) at night); in order to be able to take cuttings keep at 10–20°C (50–68°F) in winter

💧   Keep the soil moderately damp; water regularly to ensure that the soil-ball will not dry out

🗎   Tolerant of normal living-room conditions

🥛   Chalky soil mixture

Cephalocereus

Old man cactus

Even the smallest seedlings of *Cephalocereus senilis*, or Old man cactus, are already white-haired. To keep the hair clean place some pebbles on the soil

Inadequate humidity in summer frequently leads to an attack by mealy bud and red spider. Draught must be avoided at all costs. The 'Old man' will flower only in its native Mexico, for the pink flowers do not appear until the cactus reaches a height of 6m (20ft) or more. It can be grown from seed, thinly covered in finely sifted sandy soil.

☼ Requires plenty of sun

🌡 Warm (16–20°C (61–68°F) at night); in winter the temperature must not drop below 15°C (59°F)

💧 Water moderately in summer; keep dry in winter. Give a dose of special cactus fertiliser fortnightly

 Requires a somewhat humid atmosphere. In summer occasional misting advisable, but do not spray the plant itself

🪴 Standard or somewhat chalky soil mixture

Cereus

Hedge cactus

The best known species, *Cereus peruvianum* (photograph, centre), comes from the south-eastern regions of South America and is extremely vigorous. To the right you see the 'Monstrosus' variety; its strange shape is caused by a disturbance in the growing point which leads to the constant production of new tips. The cactus shown on the left is *Cereus neotetragonus*.

Most *Cereus* species flower at an advanced age, but in *Cereus chalybaeus* flowers may be produced by relatively young plants, about 50cm (20in) tall.

Propagation is from cuttings (leave them to dry before planting) or from seed.

☼ A well-lit, sunny position to induce growth

🌡 Warm (16–20°C (61–68°F) at night); cool (minimum of 3°C (37°F) in winter)

💧 Water sparingly. From time to time spray the plant to remove dust, enabling the pores to breathe

 Low humidity acceptable

🪴 Standard or chalky mixture

Ceropegia

Hearts entangled

This small succulent is an almost ideal house plant—as the instructions below will demonstrate. The *Ceropegia woodii* produces unusual pinkish flowers which have inspired the plant's name (*kēros* = wax).

In thriving plants, small cormlets develop in the axils of the marbled, fleshy leaves; these may be used to grow new plants. Ordinary cuttings will also strike readily, provided the cut surface is first allowed to dry. Plants may be grown from seed as well.

Fortnightly feeding is desirable.

☼ Tolerates both sun and semi-shade

🌡 Moderate (10–16°C (61–68°F) at night); preferably kept cool in winter, although it may be left in the living-room

💧 Water sparingly throughout the year

༄ Very tolerant of dry air

🪣 Light soil, rich in humus and with some chalk; or equal parts of standard potting compost and coarse sand

Chamaecereus

This cactus is cultivated on a large scale; properly cared for it will flower profusely. A first requirement is the correct amount of light.

For up to a week the scarlet flowers of *Chamaecereus silvestrii* will close at night and re-open in the morning. To increase the plant a section is broken off, the wound is allowed to dry and the cutting is set in a sandy mixture. It will root fairly easily. Growing from seed also presents few problems.

Re-potting is particularly difficult for the runners are very fragile.

☼ Good light, but not too much sun

🌡 Moderate (10–16°C (61–68°F) at night); should definitely be kept cool in winter—will even tolerate frost

💧 Water regularly but sparingly in summer; keep dry in winter

༄ Low humidity

🪣 Light but rich soil, containing humus and some chalk

Chamaedorea

The popularity of *Chamaedorea elegans*, a native of Mexico, is in part due to its interesting inflorescence, consisting of small yellow balls which may develop into berries. The 'Bella' strain is the smallest. Propagation is either by division, in which case rooting may present problems, or from seed. Germination may take a long time, for the large seeds are very hard. Prick out in warm conditions and for the first two years keep in a shady, humid and warm environment. The foliage should be rinsed regularly with lime-free water.

- ☼ No direct sun, but good light
- 🌡 Moderate (10–16°C (61–68°F) at night); maximum night temperature in winter 14°C (57°F)
- 💧 Water liberally in summer; plunge once a week. In winter water sparingly
- 💦 Moderate humidity; spray
- 🥄 Slightly calcereous soil, porous and rich in humus

Chamaerops

Fan palm

This is the only palm which grows wild in Europe, where *Chamaerops humilis* may grow to 5m (16ft). In a tub in the living-room it will rarely exceed 1m (3ft) but will be of spreading habit. Its typical fan-shaped foliage undoubtedly makes it a valuable asset in interior decorating. It is not difficult to grow from seed. Young plants are potted in a loamy mixture rich in humus and must be kept out of direct sunlight. Within about two years you will have a fine plant.

In winter it may be placed in a relatively dark position.

- ☼ May be placed in a sunny spot in summer
- 🌡 Moderate (10–16°C (50–61°F) at night); keep cool but frostfree in winter. Provide ventilation
- 💧 Water freely in summer; in winter keep moderately moist. Feed weekly
- 💦 Normal humidity; in summer the plant may be put out of doors
- 🥄 Somewhat chalky soil, rich in humus

Chlorophytum

Spider plant

The variegated form *Chlorophytum comosum* 'Variegatum' illustrated has an all-green relation, *Chlorophytum capense*.

To prevent the former losing its colouring, make sure it receives adequate light and not too much water or fertiliser—no need to fear that your plant may go short, for it has tubers in which reserve food is stored. Propagation is easy. Small white flowers appear at the end of long stems; these develop into small plantlets which can be detached and potted separately. Another method of propagation is by division.

☀ Tolerates sun as well as shade

🌡 Moderate (10–16°C (50–61°F) at night) or warm (16–20°C (61–68°F) at night)

💧 In summer water normally to freely; a little less in winter

💦 Reasonably tolerant of dry air, but enjoys being sprayed from time to time

🪣 Standard or somewhat loamy potting compost

Chrysanthemum

Chrysanthemum indicum hybrids have degenerated into so-called year-round plants. It is possible to market them throughout the year by utilising the fact that they are short-day plants: they flower when the days grow shorter—that is, in nature, in the autumn. By means of adjusting artificial light, flowering plants may be obtained at any time of the year. In addition, growth is inhibited by artificial means in order to produce compact and free-flowering plants. Altogether an artificial plant.

Placed in the garden after flowering it may grow to its normal proportions.

☀ Half-shady situation

🌡 Moderate (10–16°C (50–61°F) at night); can survive the winter at 4–6°C (39–43°F)

💧 Water moderately freely; make sure the soil-ball does not dry out

💦 Reasonably tolerant of dry air

🪣 Somewhat chalky to standard potting compost

Cissus

There are not a great number of truly indestructible house plants—popularly called house weeds. In addition to the universally known *Ficus*, the *Monstera* or Swiss cheese plant and the *Sansevieria*—all, of course, to be found in this book—two such plants are illustrated here. Of these *Cissus rhombifolia* (right), more often referred to as *Rhoicissus*, is undoubtedly the stronger.

Whenever in a dark room, at an incredible distance from a window, I encounter a dark green foliage plant desperately reaching for the light it is almost certain to be a *Cissus rhombifolia*. This does not mean that you should now immediately transfer yours to the windowsill—no need to overdo it. It does enjoy a moderate temperature, but in this respect, too, it is adaptable. This species may even flower (though rather inconspicuously).

The common *Cissus antarctica* (centre) is slightly less hardy; it produces large, undivided foliage instead of the triple leaves of the former species. This plant is less tolerant of dry air and occasionally presents problems in cultivation. For the sake of completeness we show *Cissus discolor* (left), a magnificent foliage plant which will, however, thrive only in a greenhouse or a flower window.

Somewhat easier to grow, but even rarer, is *Cissus striata*, a hanging plant with small, fivefold leaves. This plant should on no account be kept in too warm a position.

All *Cissus* species belong to the vine family and consequently prefer chalky, porous soil. They may be pruned.

Cuttings root easily, especially in some degree of bottom heat.

Other member of the family are described under *Ampelopsis*, *Rhoicissus* and *Tetrastigma*.

☼ Will thrive in well-lit as well as in dark positions, depending on the species

🌡 Moderate (10–16°C (50–61°F) at night); minimum temperature in winter 80C (46°F)

◊ Water moderately

〰 Humidity depending on species

▼ Chalky mixture; standard potting compost is definitely too acid

Citrus

Orange tree

The ornamental form of the edible orange is called *Citrus microcarpa* (see illustration). If it bears fruit when you buy it, it should be placed in a very well-lit spot, but not too warm. A low temperature in winter will encourage flowering. If possible place out of doors in the sun in late May; water freely and feed from time to time. The flowers will develop into fruits; however, these will turn orange very slowly. It may take as much as a year before they attain the correct colour.

Propagation is in spring from young tip cuttings set in bottom heat.

☼ Sun or light shade; in summer out of doors as much as possible, either in the garden or on the balcony

🌡 Moderate (10–16°C (50–61°F) at night); cool in winter

◊ Water freely in summer; in winter the soil-ball should be kept moist

〰 Moderate humidity

⊔ Somewhat chalky mixture

Cleistocactus

This is a large genus of tall, often white-haired cacti, which may bear narrow, elongated flowers at the top. Before they do so the plant must grow to 50–100cm (20–40in) in height, depending on the species. Unlike most other cacti, *Cleistocactus* species do not have to be kept absolutely dry in winter, nor need the temperature be below 15°C (59°F). A humid atmosphere in spring and summer is much appreciated.

The plants are best grown from seed, but cuttings may be taken as well.

The form illustrated is *Cleistocactus strausii* var. *jujuvensis*.

☼ Well-lit, sunny position throughout the year

🌡 Warm (16–20°C (61–68°F) at night); keep cool in winter

◊ In summer water moderately but adequately. Do not keep entirely dry in winter

〰 Dislikes dry air

⊔ Somewhat chalky soil

Clerodendrum

The *Clerodendrum thomsoniae*, sometimes called *Clerodendron*, is a climber best suited to a moderately warm greenhouse, where the stems may grow to 4m (13ft). By timely pruning and by pinching out the tips it may be grown into a compact house plant. If generously sprayed it will keep for a long time, especially in summer. At the end of the autumn (early December) the plant is best placed in a cool position and watered very sparingly. Towards the end of February it should be drastically cut back and re-potted. Once the plant starts into growth it should be given a warmer spot. The long shoots should be supported.

Propagation from cuttings, warm.

☼   A well-lit situation, but not in the sun

🌡   Moderate (12–16°C (54–61°F) at night); in winter keep at approximately 10–12°C (50–54°F)

💧   Keep constantly moist

🌫   Fairly high degree of humidity; the foliage should frequently be sprayed

🪴   Chalky mixture

Cleyera

Cleyera japonica is sometimes—incorrectly—called *Eurya japonica*. The green-leaved species has a white inflorescence and red fruits. The 'Tricolor' strain is grown chiefly for its fine foliage; it rarely flowers.

The *Cleyera* may be increased from tip cuttings, which require extra bottom heat to root successfully. To achieve a well-shaped plant it should occasionally have the tips removed. Re-potting is best done in spring; do not forget to press the soil down well. Feed with a lime-free fertiliser. From time to time spray with tepid water.

☼   Keep out of the sun, but in good light. May be placed out of doors in summer

🌡   Moderate (10–16°C (50–61°F) at night); keep cool in winter at about 10°C (50°F)

💧   Water moderately throughout the year, using soft water. Be careful not to let the soil-ball dry out

🌫   Moderate; spray occasionally

🪴   Standard potting compost

Clivia

The *Clivia miniata* illustrated is a most popular and attractive plant which makes few demands on its owner. The plant puts out clear signals when its care leaves something to be desired. Yellow spots on the leaves indicate either too much water or water in the heart of the plant. In too dark a position the leaves will split vertically. If no flower-stem appears it means that you have watered too freely from October onwards. The plant has to be goaded into flowering by being kept dry. After October the soil should only just be kept moist until the flower-stalk reaches 15cm (6in) then water normally. The plant may now have a slightly warmer position.

 Semi-shade; may be placed out of doors in summer

 Moderate (10–16°C (50–61°F) at night); in winter the temperature must not exceed 12–15°C (54–59°F)

 Water fairly freely in summer, but avoid stagnant water in the pot. In winter keep as dry as possible

 Moderate humidity, but dry air is tolerated

 Compost-based soil

Codiaeum

Croton

One is constantly amazed at the enormous variety which occurs in the marking and colouring of the foliage of *Codiaeum variegatum* var. *pictum*. The plant is a native of Eastern Asia. To maintain its fine colouring it should be given adequate light and air. Dry air may cause the leaves to drop, or lead to mildew, red spider and thrips. Regular spraying and/or placing the pot in a water-filled dish will help.

Propagation is from mature shoots, which will strike at a high bottom temperature. Rooting powder should be applied first. Root under glass or plastic in light soil, at a temperature of 25–30°C (77–86°F).

 Sun or light shade

 Warm (16–20°C (61–68°F) at night); 16–18°C (61–64°F) in winter

 Keep fairly moist in spring and summer; less in winter. The soil-ball must not be allowed to dry out

 Beware of dry air; spray regularly

 Mixture of leafmould and moorland soil

Coelogyne

Among the two hundred *Coelogyne* species *Coelogyne cristata* is perfectly suitable for living-room cultivation. Some other species which may successfully be grown in a moderate greenhouse or in the living-room are *Coelogyne dayana*, *C. massangeana* and *C. pandurata*. All these orchids have a dormant season in winter, when less water should be given for 6–8 weeks. At night the temperature should not drop below 12°C (54°F). After flowering—in *Coelogyne cristata* the flowers are creamy-white with yellow-crested lips and appear from January to April—the plants may be re-potted either in special orchid baskets or in pots filled to a third of their depth with crocks.

☼   Semi-shade is best

🌡   Warm (16–20°C (61–68°F) at night); in winter 14–16°C (57–61°F) is adequate

💧   Water fairly freely, using demineralised and lime-free water. Water only sparingly in December

💨   High degree of humidity. When spraying beware of staining the petals

🪣   Special orchid mixture

Coleus

Flame nettle

Easily grown from cuttings, few special requirements, rapid growth and a cheerful appearance —all these characteristics explain the popularity of the *Coleus*. The forms most frequently grown are the multicoloured Blumei hybrids (photograph, right), which have an upright habit and whose leaves are larger than those of *Coleus pumilus* with its recumbent stems.

It is not worth keeping flame nettles through the winter, although you might keep one plant to take cuttings in spring. Tip shoots will root in water in a dark bottle, as well as in seed compost (lime-free). The plants may also be grown from seed in February–March.

☼   Because of its colouring the plant must be placed in the best possible light, possibly full sun

🌡   Moderately warm (14–18°C (57–64°F) at night)

💧   In summer water freely, using soft water (pH 4–4.5). Plunge at least once a week

💨   Reasonably high degree of humidity; spray frequently, particularly when the temperature is high

🪣   Loamy soil rich in humus, or standard potting compost

Columnea

Both *Columnea microphylla* (the variegated form, lower photograph) and *Columnea hirta* are epiphytes originating in Costa Rica. They prefer a mixture of coarse moorland soil and leaf-mould, with sphagnum moss and a few pieces of charcoal. In the flowering season be generous with organic liquid fertiliser. Flowering will be more profuse if you keep the plant in a somewhat cooler environment and water more sparingly in winter.

After flowering the plant must be pruned, for *Columnea* flowers on the new shoots: the shape of the plant and the distribution of the flowers will also benefit and, as an extra bonus, cuttings may be taken from the prunings. This is best done in March–May. The cuttings, about 10cm (4in) in length, are placed in a mixture of equal parts of peat and sand and kept at a minimum temperature of 20°C (68°F) until they are well rooted (this takes 2–3 weeks). Transfer in groups of three or four to fairly shallow pots and, once the little plants are growing well, pinch out the tips to encourage bushy growth. Ensure a high degree of humidity by using the water-filled bowl method or an evaporator. During the growing period give a lime-free feed once a week.

Among the two hundred *Columnea* species —they are clearly related to *Aeschynanthus*, pp. 28–29—the following are most suited to living-room cultivation. *Columnea × banksii* has scarlet, two-lipped flowers and drooping or creeping stems with small oval leaves; it flowers in spring. *Columnea gloriosa* has trailing stems with rounded oval leaves, hairy and green to reddish-brown (in 'Purpurea'), and orange-red flowers with a yellow throat. *Columnea × kewensis* is semi-erect in habit; at a later stage the stems will droop. *Columnea microphylla* is a smaller species and *Columnea schiedeana* is a climber.

 Hang or place in slight shade

 Warm (16–20°C (61–68°F) at night); in the autumn keep at 10–15°C (50–59°F), in winter at 15–18°C (59–64°F)

 Keep the soil moist, using tepid, soft water

 Constant, fairly high degree of humidity

 Friable mixture, rich in humus and with sphagnum added

Cordyline

This tropical plant with its magnificent foliage must be kept warm and moist. Dropping foliage and yellowing leaf-tips indicate inadequate humidity. The *Cordyline terminalis* illustrated is among the most delicate species and should spend the winter at 10–13°C (50–55°F). In summer feed every fortnight. Re-pot every second or third year in April–May.

When a *Cordyline* loses its lower leaves it may be air-layered. New plants may be grown from tip cuttings or stem sections with at least three eyes. Dip in rooting powder and keep the bottom temperature at 26–30°C (79–86°F). It can also be grown from seed sown in February.

☼   Fairly good light, but will tolerate some shade

🌡   Warm (16–20°C (61–68°F) at night); temperature in winter 4–7°C (39–45°F)

💧   Soil-ball must be neither too dry nor too wet

   Constant, high degree of humidity essential

🪣   Standard potting compost

Cotyledon

This genus of succulents embraces about fifty species and can be divided into evergreen and deciduous groups. Among the latter are *Cotyledon paniculata* and *Cotyledon reticulata*, which must be kept dry until the first small leaves appear in the late fall. Of the other group *Cotyledon orbiculata* and *Cotyledon undulata* (illustrated) are the best known species. Both have bloomed leaves and orange-red flowers, but *Cotyledon orbiculata* grows much larger.

A good soil mixture may be obtained by combining equal parts of sand, loam and leaf-mould. Propagation is from cuttings in summer, or from seed.

☼   Sunny position

🌡   Warm (16–20°C (61–68°F) at night); temperature in winter about 10°C (50°F)

💧   Water sparingly; the leaves must not get wet. Deciduous species must be kept dry when the leaves have dropped

   Low degree of humidity is sufficient

🪣   Special mixture, friable and acid

Crassula

This genus comprises three hundred succulents, most of which originate in the Cape Province. Like most other succulents they require a sunny position, low humidity, little water and a loamy, porous soil mixture. A low temperature in winter prevents lanky growth, attack by aphids, and loss of foliage.

Propagation is from tip or leaf cuttings. Always allow the cutting to dry a little in the shade before rooting it in a mixture of equal parts of sand and peat. New plants may also be grown from seed; this will usually germinate in two weeks. Re-pot in March when the plant puts forth new shoots. Special cactus mixture is suitable as well.

The upper photograph shows, from left to right: *Crassula portulacea*, which has stumpy, shiny green leaves, branches freely and may grow to a height of a metre, rarely flowering; *Crassula lycopodioides*, which grows to about 25cm (10in) and has small white flowers; and *Crassula crenulata*, whose inflorescence consists of red umbels.

On the left in the lower photograph you see *Crassula perforata*, with grey-green triangular, opposite-growing leaves, joined at the bottom. The inflorescence is yellow, 3–6cm (1–2½in) in length. In the background, right is *Crassula rotundifolia* which, as the name indicates, has circular leaves, grey-green in colour, often merging into pink along the margin. The flowers are yellow. In the foreground, right, is *Crassula marginalis rubra*, very suitable because of its drooping stems, to be grown as a hanging plant. This species has small, heart-shaped leaves, slightly reddish in colour. The small white flowers provide added decoration.

☼ Do not place in full sun; in late May it may be placed outside in a sheltered position

🌡 Warm (10–16°C (50–61°F) at night); a temperature of 6–12°C (43–54°F) in winter encourages flowering

💧 Water sparingly throughout the year; in winter keep practically dry

〰 Low degree of humidity

🪣 Sandy, porous mixture, rich in humus

Crocus

It is not difficult to bring crocuses into flower indoors. Suitable bulbs are potted in October and, if possible, buried in a spot in the garden which will not be too hard to dig in January (protect with dead leaves or straw). A cool cellar will do equally well, provided the bulbs are kept in total darkness. During this period water sparingly. As soon as the buds can be felt, the containers may be brought into the light. Be sure not to place them in too warm a position and keep the atmosphere moist by spraying or—another good method—by half-covering the noses with a plastic bag.

☼ Semi-shade

🌡 Cool (3–10°C (37–50°F) at night)

💧 Water moderately; too much water may cause root-rot

💦 Fairly high degree of humidity essential; this may be provided by mist-spraying from time to time

🍵 Somewhat chalky potting compost

Crossandra

Unless you are able to provide adequate humidity, this is not an easy plant to grow. In a greenhouse, an enclosed flower window, or in combination with other plants in a large container, it will present few problems, but in a pot by itself on the windowsill it will not be a success, especially when the central heating is on.

It can be kept from one season to another only if placed in a slightly cooler environment, and watered somewhat less, in the dormant season. It is better to take cuttings; these will root in spring in bottom heat. Place a few together in one pot. The plant's full name is *Crossandra infundibuliformis*, 'funnel-shaped'.

☼ Semi-shade in summer; good light in winter, but not in full sun

🌡 Warm (16–20°C (61–68°F) at night); in winter the temperature must not drop below 12°C (54°F)

💧 Water freely in the growing season, using soft water

💦 High degree of humidity essential

🍵 Light mixture, rich in humus

Cryptanthus

The attractive multi-coloured plants illustrated on this page are all bromeliads—this is, rosette-shaped plants which die after flowering. In these plants the inflorescence is in any case inconspicuous, and as a rule numerous new rosettes develop next to the old one, so that it is hardly noticeable when the plant is dying.

To keep these plants in good condition for several years on end a heated greenhouse is almost essential, but, provided they are kept out of the sun, they will keep successfully in the living-room for quite a long time, especially in summer when the heating is off. It is advisable to combine several plants in a shallow pottery bowl.

The upper photograph shows, left, *Cryptanthus acaulis* and, right, the very striking *Cryptanthus bromelioides* 'Tricolor'. The third leaf colour, pink, will appear only if the plants are placed in good light.

In the lower photograph you see, left, *Cryptanthus bivittatus* and, right, the well-known *Cryptanthus zonatus* 'Zebrinus' with its unusual marking. When buying one of the latter, search until you find a good specimen, for often the marking has become blurred as a result of inadequate light. (In flowershops without a greenhouse showroom, many plants have a hard time.)

Although in the wild most bromeliads grow on trees, *Cryptanthus* may be found at ground-level as well, and because of this normal potting compost may be added to the special bromeliad soil. It does not mind too much if it is temporarily kept dry. In winter it may be watered even more sparingly than in summer. If you are able to provide a little extra humidity in summer, the plant will undoubtedly be grateful. From time to time put a little foliage fertiliser in the spray.

Propagation is by removing young rosettes together with some roots.

☼ Slightly shady position

🌡 Warm (16–20°C (61–68°F) at night); high temperature in winter: 20–22°C (68–72°F)

💧 Water very sparingly, but do not allow the soil-ball to dry out

💨 High degree of humidity required

🪣 Porous mixture, rich in humus, e.g. containing leaf-mould and sphagnum

Ctenanthe

This cheerful foliage plant has proved to be fairly hardy and has therefore become more in demand in recent years. It is particularly suitable for plant containers in a warm room, for among other plants the air is somewhat more humid. To maintain the foliage marking, plenty of light is desirable, though less light is tolerated also. *Ctenanthe* (usually pronounced 'Stenanthe') develops a spreading root system and therefore does best in shallow containers or in the garden. The species illustrated is *Ctenanthe lubbersiana. Ctenanthe oppenheimiana* 'Variegata' has more pointed leaves and very clear marking.

- ☼ Semi-shade
- 🌡 Warm (16–20°C (61–68°F) at night); in winter a daytime temperature of 18–20°C (64–68°F) is sufficient
- ◊ Keep moderately moist, using soft water (pH 4.5)
- 💦 Syringe regularly to keep the air humid
- ⛏ Leafmould mixed with peat and cow manure

Cuphea

Mexican cigar flower

Cuphea ignea, a plant with bright red tubular flowers, is usually grown from seed and brought on the market in full flower. It may be placed outside in the sun.

  If you want to keep a plant through the winter, it must be kept cool and watered very sparingly. In February–March cuttings may be rooted in some degree of bottom heat; these will soon develop into mature plants. Place a few together in a pot. As a rule the mother plant will not flower as well as the new plants.

- ☼ Well-lit, sunny spot; the plant enjoys fresh air
- 🌡 Moderate (10–16°C (50–61°F) at night); keep cool but frostfree in winter
- ◊ Maintain constant moisture
- 💦 Normal living-room atmosphere is sufficiently humid
- ⛏ Somewhat chalky potting compost

Cyclamen

To keep the *Cyclamen persicum* in good condition it should constantly be borne in mind that the grower always cultivates this plant in a cool environment. If it is suddenly transferred to a warm room the leaves will soon droop and no amount of watering will counteract this—on the contrary, excess moisture may cause the corm to rot, and of course this kills the plant.

The secret therefore is to keep the temperature at 10–16°C (50–61°F) and to pour tepid water into the saucer every second day, removing the excess after fifteen minutes. If your house is single-glazed, the temperature near a north-facing window will be approximately right in November, provided, of course, that your windowsill is wide enough to keep the plant out of the air rising from the central heating radiator, if you have one there. You would do well to check the temperature. If nevertheless the foliage droops, either because of the temperature or through lack of water, plunge the plant immediately.

If is perfectly possible to keep a cyclamen from year to year. After flowering decrease the water supply until all the leaves have faded. Leave the pot for about a month and then re-pot the corm in a slightly larger pot in fresh potting compost, preferably with a little clay added. Water sparingly to bring the corm into growth; be sure to keep cool. Occasionally give some fertiliser.

In summer—from mid-May onwards, but beware of night frost—the cyclamen may be grown in a sheltered, shady spot in the garden.

The upper photograph shows a pink and a red cyclamen, both commonly available. Some strains have fringed flower petals. Below you see a small-flowered, fragrant cyclamen with a very natural appearance.

Cyclamens may be grown from seed under glass, at a temperature of 15–20°C (59–68°F)

☼ Some shade required; in bright sunlight the plants will quickly droop

🌡 Cold (3–10°C (37–50°F) at night)

◊ During the flowering season water fairly freely, using soft, tepid water

💨 Fairly high degree of humidity; the leaves should be frequently sprayed

🥛 Potting compost with a little extra clay

Cyperus

Umbrella plant

Fine large specimens of the umbrella plant are greatly in demand, because the plant is very hardy as well as decorative. Most species are not very demanding as regards light and temperature. As far as watering is concerned, the rule is always to keep it soaking wet. Other plants would suffer, but the *Cyperus* revels in it. The best known species is *Cyperus alternifolius*, which grows to 1–1.5m (3–5ft). Narrow-leaved 'umbrellas' arise on tall stems; the plant rarely flowers. *Cyperus gracilis* (photograph, left) is very similar, but smaller in all respects; it rarely exceeds 40cm (16in) in height and is therefore more suitable for the windowsill.

The plant shown on the right in the photograph is *Cyperus diffusus*, a low-growing species with fairly wide leaves; it flowers readily. The most decorative species (which is, however, also the most difficult to grow) is the paper reed, from which the ancient Egyptians made their famous papyrus. This is actually a hot-house plant, found in every botanical garden. It is occasionally grown successfully indoors; the stems may then grow to 2m (6ft). The leaves are very narrow; and it has a drooping, radiating inflorescence. It is best placed in a very large plant community, where it must, however, have its own container, constantly filled with water.

All umbrella plants dislike excessively dry air. They should never be placed above a radiator; better to put them on the floor. Glass tanks are very suitable; after planting cover the soil with a layer of attractive white pebbles.

Cyperus is very easily increased, and this may be done in several ways. It may be when it is being re-potted. When taking cuttings use the young tip-shoots with about 5cm (2in) of the stem. Cut the leaves back to half their size and root in damp sand.

☼ Slight shade

🌡 Moderate (10–16°C (50–61°F) at night; in winter preferably 10–12°C (50–54°F), but may be kept in a heated room

◊ Permanent footbath required; abundant water and spraying essential

〽 Fairly high degree of humidity desirable

🪣 Slightly chalky mixture; the plant is not demanding

Cyrtomium

Holly fern

Not nearly as well known as the Hart's horn fern (see under *Platycerium*) or the *Pellaea*, this is nevertheless very suitable for plant troughs, especially those in cool places such as entrance halls, corridors, etc. In a lower temperature the air will automatically be more humid, and this is what the holly fern enjoys. It is very undemanding where light is concerned: before the foliage has become entirely dark green even darker positions are acceptable. The species photographed is *Cyrtomium falcatum*. Feed generously, especially in summer, encouraging leaf development.

☼ Satisfied with little light

🌡 Moderate (10–16°C (50–61°F) at night); in winter the temperature may drop to 10°C (50°F)

💧 Water freely in the growing season; in winter keep moderately moist

💨 Requires a fairly high degree of humidity; regular misting necessary

🪣 Chalky, humusy potting compost

Cytisus

Broom

Where heating engineers gained ground, the good old broom lost it, for the most favourable temperatures for this plant are between 12 and 18°C (54–64°F). If you possess a room which always remains reasonably cool, the plant may be kept through the winter without problems. Decrease the water supply in proportion to the lowering temperature. Flowers appear fairly early in spring. Provided it is frequently sprayed, the broom may be transferred to the warm living-room. After flowering it can be cut back a little; it is then re-potted. Propagation is from cuttings.

The plant illustrated is *Cytisus × racemosus*.

☼ In summer a sunny spot out of doors; a little shade in winter

🌡 Cool (3–10°C (37–50°F) at night); must be kept cool in winter: 4–8°C (39–46°F)

💧 When in flower water normally; sparingly in winter

💨 Moderate humidity

🪣 Calcareous potting compost

Dendrobium

Nearly all the species of this fine orchid prefer to grow in a well-lit, heated greenhouse. *Dendrobium nobile* may be cultivated in the living-room, but in winter a complete rest, without water and at about 10°C (50°F), is essential. *Dendrobium thyrsiflorum*, another strong species, requires a slightly higher temperature and a less pronounced drought in the dormant season; it does not lose all its leaves.

All orchids should be given only lime-free water; also remember the special soil mixture required. The form illustrated is the greenhouse plant *Dendrobium zeno × ceylon* 'Glory'. For further details consult a book on orchids.

☼ Requires a very well-lit position

🌡 Warm (16–20°C (61–68°F) at night); cool in winter or warm throughout the year, depending on the species

◊ Water moderately

🌫 Higher or lower degree of humidity depending on the species

🪴 One part sphagnum, two parts fern roots

Didymochlaena

This fern, with its difficult name, is by no means rare. The photograph shows *Didymochlaena trunculata*, which has double-pinnate brownish leaves and is very satisfactory in plant troughs in a not too warm position in winter. Ensure that the soil-ball never dries out entirely; this would cause the foliage to drop. Re-pot at the end of winter; cut back a little and place the plant in a warmer spot to bring it into growth. The use of plastic pots is advisable. Feed fairly generously in the growing season. Propagation is by division or from spores, which ripen indoors.

☼ Will thrive in a shady position

🌡 Warm (16–20°C (61–68°F) at night); keep cool in winter (14–16°C (57–61°F))

◊ In the growing season water freely, using soft water (pH 5)

🌫 In summer mist-spray several times a day; do not spray in winter

🪴 Potting compost rich in humus

Dieffenbachia

These striking, evergreen foliage plants, originating in tropical regions of the Americas, have in recent years become firmly entrenched on our windowsills, and especially in plant containers. They have proved to be quite adaptable to the characteristically dry atmosphere of centrally heated houses. Nevertheless the best results will be achieved by frequently spraying the foliage or providing a higher degree of humidity by some other means (evaporator, air conditioning). *Dieffenbachia* does not really enjoy the temperatures of our living-rooms and offices.

Some confusion exists in the naming of the various species. The best known is called *Dieffenbachia seguine*. The leaves are of an elongated oval shape, 20–40cm (8–16in) in length, 10–20cm (4–8in) wide, and are always shiny with variegated marking. Various forms are available. 'Rudolph Roehrs' is very pale yellow-green, with dark margins and central veins. A hybrid called 'Arvida' (or 'Exotica') has matt green foliage with very irregular white mottling (upper photograph). The biggest and thickest leaves, on a thick trunk, are produced by *Dieffenbachia amoena* (lower photograph); they are up to 80cm (30in) in length and the plants grow to 1m (40in). There is also *Dieffenbachia × bausei*, distinguished by its marbled leaf-stalk and rather rectangular leaves, and *Dieffenbachia bowmannii*, also matt green, but larger leaves.

The juice of *Dieffenbachia* contains strychnine and is therefore very poisonous. Few people eat their house plants, but there is a known instance of a drunkard biting into a *Dieffenbachia* and suffering severe poisoning.

Propagation from tip-shoots rooted under glass. Bare plants may but cut back drastically; as a rule they will then put forth new shoots

☼ Semi-shade, never direct sunlight

🌡 Warm (16–20°C (61–68°F) at night); in winter the temperature must not drop below 15–18°C (59–64°F)

💧 In summer water fairly freely, using soft, tepid water; the soil-ball must not dry out

🌫 Fairly humid atmosphere required throughout the year, provided by frequent misting

🪣 Standard to chalky potting compost

Dionaea

Venus fly-trap

In recent years this plant has become freely available at the florists' or at flower markets. It is an amusing insectivore, but is not easy to keep in good condition. *Dionaea muscipula* is actually a greenhouse plant, requiring a very humid atmosphere. It is therefore best grown in a glass case, an indoor greenhouse, under a glass dome, etc., but certainly not in too dark a spot. Probably the greatest problem is that the plant must be kept cool. Although it may grow well in a warm environment it will usually not survive for long.

The plant can be increased by division, from leaf cuttings or from seed.

☼ Well-lit, sunny position; on very hot days provide some shade

🌡 Cool (3–10°C (37–50°F) at night); in winter keep cool but frostfree

💧 Water fairly freely; make sure that the soil-ball does not dry out

💨 High degree of humidity required

🪴 Peat soil

Dipladenia

Dipladenia is by nature a greenhouse plant and has a difficult time in the dry atmosphere of a living-room. Nevertheless a plant kept in my neighbour's living-room had twenty flowers all at one time, so it is worth trying. Of course the most difficult problem is to provide the correct winter temperature—see the symbols below. Frequently spray the foliage, cut back a little in spring, re-pot it and—who knows?— it may flower again. Propagate from cuttings in bottom heat and under glass.

The plant illustrated is *Dipladenia sanderi* 'Rosea'; this is the strongest of the hybrids.

☼ Requires a fair amount of light, but does not tolerate direct sunlight

🌡 Warm (16–20°C (61–68°F) at night); in January and February keep a little cooler (12–15°C (54–59°F)); otherwise 18°C (64°F)

💧 Water normally in summer, a little less in the dormant season

💨 High degree of humidity required

🪴 Standard to loamy potting soil

Dipteracanthus

There are innumerable small, tropical, multi-coloured foliage plants which cannot live on the windowsill but are very suitable for planting in a glass case, bottle gardens, flower windows, etc. One of these is the *Dipteracanthus devosianus* illustrated. A humid atmosphere is a prerequisite. Grow the plant in a warm environment throughout the year; in the growing season provide some nutrition and take cuttings when the plant becomes unsightly. These will root under glass in bottom heat.

This plant is frequently sold under the name *Ruellia*. Among its well known relatives is the *Fittonia* (p.92).

☼   Semi-shade or diffused sunlight

🌡   Warm (16–20°C (61–68°F) at night)

💧   Water regularly; soil should be constantly moist

💨   Fairly high degree of humidity, provided by adequate misting

🪣   Potting compost rich in humus

Dizygotheca

Finger aralia

The Finger aralia must be grown in a fairly warm environment. The photograph shows the ordinary *Dizygotheca elegantissima*, with its narrow leaves, and the relatively rare *Dizygotheca veitchii*, which put forth wider and shorter leaves of a deeper green. Both species require a fairly humid atmosphere and will therefore as a rule give disappointment if placed on the windowsill. Once it was discovered that there are many much hardier house plants, the cultivation of these species decreased considerably. You might try one in an entrance hall or a corridor.

Propagation is from seed.

☼   Well-lit, but out of direct sunlight

🌡   Moderate (10–16°C (50–61°F) at night) for older plants; slightly warmer for younger specimens; not below 15°C (59°F) even in winter

💧   Water moderately (pH 5–6)

💨   Requires a fairly humid atmosphere

🪣   Standard proprietary potting soil

Dracaena

In these two pages we devote our full attention to *Dracaena* species, house plants which are beginning to occupy an increasingly important position—and rightly so, for not only are they most decorative, they also possess amazing powers of resistance, are almost impossible to kill and are satisfied with little light. As you have read earlier in this book, larger specimens are capable of creating a very agreeable atmosphere in offices and living-rooms. They may be left undisturbed for years on end.

There are numerous species, most of which have been used as house plants for nearly a century. *Dracaena deremensis* (this page, upper photograph) originates in tropical Africa, where it must surely grow like a weed, for even in the living-room it displays an impressive love of life. Like most *Dracaena* species this plant develops a strong trunk, ending in a shock of leaves. In the variety 'Bausei' a broad white stripe runs down the grey-green leaf; 'Warneckii' (illustrated) has narrow white lines along the margin.

Dracaena draco, the dragon tree—in Tenerife and other places specimens a thousand years old have been found—will do well in the living-room, but is rarely available. The leaf rosettes are plain dark green. This plant is easily grown from seed. In winter it may be kept in a cool spot (10°C (50°F)).

Dracaena fragrans (this page, lower photograph) already took pride of place in our grandparents' day. The leaves are broader and more rounded than in *Dracaena deremensis*; this species, too, is extremely hardy. 'Massangeana' (illustrated) has a golden central stripe on a grass-green background; 'Lindenii' has golden margins to the leaves.

The plant in the photograph is a so-called 'Ti-plant'. In some parts of the world these *Dracaenas* are grown on a large scale. After a few years the trunks, by then of quite a size, are cut down, and after the foliage has been removed they are exported dry to the United States and to Europe. If, after several months, the dry trunks—either whole or cut in sections—are planted in damp soil, they will put forth new growth. Roots develop at the bottom and within a short time a plant, several metres in height, is obtained. A high-class florist will

Dracaena (continued)

combine two or three trunks in a goodlooking tub or cylinder and will be able to charge a hefty price for the arrangement. The plants are worth the expense.

Dracaena godseffinana (this page, upper photograph) bears no resemblance to the other species. The leaves are small and mottled and do not form rosettes. This species is less well known and is, moreover, not quite so hardy.

Dracaena marginata (this page, lower photograph) will be missing from most plant books. Nevertheless this modest, narrow-leaved species is probably the hardiest of them all, nor is it all that rare. It will grow in the most unlikely dark corners. Two or three specimens of varying height are planted in one pot.

Another very strong species is *Dracaena hookeriana*, a native of South Africa; it has narrow green leaves, up to 80cm (30in) in length. There are also variegated strains, among other 'Latifolia' and 'Variegata'. *Dracaena reflexa* readily develops several trunks or branches; the white-variegated strain 'Song of India' is particularly well-known.

Dracaena sanderiana was at one time very popular, but is now seen less often. The fairly small, pointed leaves grow in rosettes and are usually bright green with a pure white margin. These plants have a much more compact habit than, for instance, *Dracaena deremensis* and are thus easily recognised.

Dracaena species can really be killed only by drowning or by too cold an environment. The danger of drowning is particularly great where the plant is set in one of the modern plastic cylinders. In some cases it is sufficient to water once a fortnight.

Do not forget to re-pot every year. Cuttings can be taken from tip-shoots, preferably in spring of course. Root them under glass, removing some or all of the leaves.

☼ Well-lit spot, but no direct sun

🌡 Warm (16–20°C (61–68°F) at night); most species like to spend the winter at 15–18°C (59–64°F)

◊ The soil-ball must not dry out, neither must it be too wet; water normally

🔅 Moderate humidity adequate

🪣 Rich, humusy potting mixture

Duchesnea

Indian strawberry

It is evident from the photograph that *Duchesnea indica* is related to the domestic strawberry, of which the botanical name is *Fragraria × ananassa*. The house plant, however, produces yellow instead of white flowers from June onwards. The attractive red berries which follow are of decorative value only. The runners of this plant are reasonably winter-hardy. Provided they are given some protection they will stand up to some degree of frost and they may therefore be kept out of doors in winter. The mother plant rarely survives.

Propagation is from runners or from seed. Sow in April in a moderately warm seedbed. Germination will follow in 3–4 weeks.

☼ In summer hang in good light either indoors or out of doors; indoors in winter

🌡 Moderate (10–16°C (50–61°F) at night); prefers to be kept cool in winter (10–12°C (50–54°F), but may remain in the living-room

💧 Freely in summer, sparingly in winter

🌢 Moderate humidity

🪣 Standard potting compost

Echeveria

In this genus of succulents the sappy leaves usually grow in rosettes, varying greatly in colour and shape, but nearly always beautiful. They are undemanding plants and it is therefore not surprising that they are popular.

The photograph on this page shows a flowering *Echeveria agavoides* (rear), a plant grown on a large scale, with (left) a so-called cristate or crest-forming variety called *Echeveria agavoides* 'Cristata'. To the right you see the blue-green rosette of *Echeveria elegans*, with the beautiful colour contrast of its inflorescence. Most species are easily brought into flower, provided they are kept cool in winter.

In summer *Echeveria* species may safely be placed out of doors; the colour of the rosettes will improve in the sun. Water reasonably freely in dry weather, but be careful with watering when the skies are cloudy. The same applies to the winter season, when you should give only just enough water to prevent the leaves from shrivelling up. Excess moisture will

Echeveria (continued)

rapidly cause root-rot.

The photograph shows, left, the hairy rosette of *Echeveria setosa*, which flowers in May–June, and, right, the slightly larger *Echeveria secunda* 'Pumila'.

Because of its numerous runners the species *Echeveria carnicolor* is sometimes used as a hanging plant. Trunk-forming species, which may grow to 70cm (28in) are—among others—*Echeveria coccinea* and *E. gibbiflora*. Propagation is by rooting young rosettes.

- ☼ A well-lit or sunny position throughout the year; in summer place the pot out of doors
- 🌡 Moderate (10–16°C (50–61°F) at night); 6–10°C (43–50°F) in winter
- 💧 Water very sparingly
- 〰 Low humidity
- ▼ Somewhat chalky, porous potting compost, rich in humus

Echinocactus

Golden ball

In Germany the most important species of this genus, *Echinocactus grusonii*, is called 'Mother-in-law's chair'. After several year of careful cultivation it may indeed attain the size of a small stool, but to achieve this it is essential to keep the cactus fairly cool in winter, since otherwise rotting may occur. In some climates it will not flower; its decorative value is then due entirely to its beautiful sharp spines. Large specimens are, of course, expensive to buy. Propagation is from imported seed. Be particularly careful when pricking out the young seedlings.

- ☼ Except in spring, may be put in the sun throughout the year
- 🌡 Warm (16–20°C (61–68°F) at night), cool in winter (8–10°C (46–50°F))
- 💧 Keep completely dry during the dormant season; water sparingly at other times
- 〰 Dry living-room atmosphere excellent
- ▼ Cactus mixture or potting compost mixed with sand and chalk

Echinocereus

On this page we are dealing with two lesser known cacti, which resemble each other in name only. The upper photograph shows *Echinocereus gentryi*, like all the species of this genus of branching habit, with round, columnar stems. There are thornless as well as spined forms. Properly cared for they will put forth magnificent, large flowers.

All-green species prefer the sunniest possible outdoor position in summer. Hairy specimens are better kept in a greenhouse or on the windowsill. A low temperature in winter will encourage flowering. Propagation from detached columns, or from seed.

☼ Plenty of light and sun throughout the year; green forms out of doors in summer

🌡 Warm (16–20°C (61–68°F) at night); keep cool in winter

💧 Keep fairly dry, especially in winter; use slightly alkaline water (pH 7–7.5)

🌦 Moderate humidity

🪴 Humus-free loamy mixture, with sand

Echinopsis

In contrast to the genus described above, these cacti are alway globular in shape. The flowers, enormous in proportion to the small body of the cactus, to some extent resemble those of the slightly better known leaf cacti (see opposite page). Many hybrids are in cultivation in addition to the original botanical species such as *Echinopsis mamillosa* (illustrated). The red, white or pale lilac flower are often fragrant and usually appear at night. With normal care, and kept cool in winter, these plants will present few problems. Propagation from seed.

☼ A sunny spot preferred

🌡 Warm (16–20°C (61–68°F at night); keep cool in winter

💧 Keep fairly dry throughout the year; withhold water in winter

🌦 Low humidity; will thrive in dry air

🪴 Requires porous, rich and somewhat chalky soil

Epiphyllum

Leaf cactus

This cactus is more often called *Phyllocactus*. The plants themselves are not very attractive, but they produce magnificent, large flowers. The hybrids, with flowers in all shade of red, purple, pink and white, are the finest. They are rarely available at the florists', but they are relatively easy to grow from cuttings or seed.

From late May onwards it is advisable to place the plants out of doors in a shady spot, not forgetting to water and feed them. Bring them back indoors towards the end of September, continue watering, but from December to February keep very dry. Gradually increase the moisture when the first buds appear.

☼ Out of the sun, but plenty of light; in summer in a sheltered outdoor position

🌡 Moderate (10–16°C (50–61°F at night); keep cool in winter at 8–10°C (46–50°F)

💧 Water freely, using tepid water (pH 4.5–5); less in the autumn; very little in winter

〰 Average humidity

🪴 Mixture of sphagnum, peat fibre and loam

Episcia

These little known foliage plants are members of the *Gesneria* family and are therefore typical hothouse plants. Nevertheless they may temporarily be given a place in plant troughs, plant cases and especially in automatically controlled flower windows. Where the temperature is not too high the plants will keep in good condition all the longer.

There are species with brown-mottled, wrinkled foliage as well as hanging plants such as the *Episcia dianthiflora* illustrated; the latter has fringed flowers. Propagation from runners rooted at a bottom temperature of at least 20°C (68°F) under glass or plastic.

☼ A shady spot, but not too dark

🌡 Warm (16–20°C (61–68°F) at night)

💧 Water regularly, keeping the soil reasonably moist

〰 High degree of humidity required, especially at high temperatures

🪴 Friable, porous leafmould; if necessary a proprietary potting compost

81

Erica

Heath

You may not be attracted by the idea of growing heath indoors; nevertheless there are a number of African species which are excellent for use in the living-room or on the balcony. As a rule they are thrown away when they have ceased flowering, but it is perfectly possible to keep them. The upper photograph shows *Erica gracilis*, a small-flowered variety available from late September onwards. It is ideal for filling window or balcony boxes, for it will continue flowering for at least two months, until a severe frost puts an end to it. This heath is also very satisfactory in a not too warm room.

Erica hiemalis (lower photograph) flowers from February onwards; the colours are white, salmon pink or rose-red. This plant is only suitable for indoors.

Erica × willmorei, found at the florist's from March onwards, produces very large, tubular flowers of a magnificent cherry-red. In summer we occasionally find the lilac-flowering *Erica ventricosa*.

All the species mentioned must be given the coolest possible position in order to last. It is therefore advisable to put them in a corridor, an entrance hall, or in a utility kitchen, provided it is well-lit and frostfree. In frostfree weather some may go out of doors, especially, as we have seen, *Erica gracilis*.

To keep the plants for another season they should be cut back a little after flowering, and in May should be planted, pot and all, in a half-shady spot in the garden. Do not forget to give sufficient water—if possible rainwater, for heath dislikes lime and as you know tapwater is now quite calciferous in many regions. Ordinary proprietary potting compost contains far too much chalk for these plants.

Propagation is from tip-cuttings in July–August, but they are not easy to grow into flowering plants.

☼ Well-lit to sunny position, especially in summer

🌡 Cold (3–10°C (37–50°F) at night); keep cool in winter (6–8°C (43–46°F))

◊ Water moderately with soft water (pH 4–4.5)

🌫 Moderate humidity

🪣 Acid, humusy soil (mixture of moorland soil, peat fibre and lime-free sand)

Espostoa

Peruvian old man

This is one of the many so-called 'old man' cacti, plants entirely covered in fine hairs as a protection against the sun. In its native Peru the *Espostoa lanata* illustrated may grow to a height of 4m (13ft), the trunk sometimes branching like a candelabra. In its native habitat, 6cm (2½in) long pale pink flowers appear at night, but in this country the plant will not flower. Indoors it may grow to a metre in height. It is advisable to spray occasionally.

The winter temperature required is considerably higher than for other cacti and it can therefore quite well be grown in the living-room. The specimen illustrated has been grafted.

☼ Always in a sunny position

🌡 Warm (16–20°C (61–68°F) at night); in winter not below 15°C (59°F)

💧 In the flowering season water fairly freely; keep dry in winter

💨 Fairly low humidity is sufficient

🪣 Cactus mixture of chalky potting compost

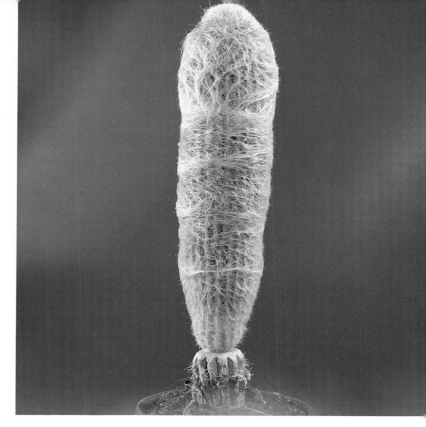

Euonymus

This pot plant is related to the garden shrub of the same name, but the indoor species rarely produces fruits. Their ornamental value is derived solely from the beautiful variegated foliage. They are not really suitable for use in the warm living-room; they thrive only in a cool position, particularly in winter. The photograph shows three variegated forms of *Euonymus japonicus*, namely, from left to right: 'Medio-Pictus', 'Albomarginatus' and 'Microphyllus-Variegatus'. There are many more variegated strains.

Propagation is from young shoots in a warm, enclosed propagator.

☼ Tolerates both sun and half-shade

🌡 Cold (3–10°C (37–50°F) at night); must be kept cool in winter; will even stand up to slight nightfrost

💧 Water regularly, a little more in early summer than during the rest of the year

💨 Moderate humidity

🪣 Potting compost rich in humus

Euphorbia milii

Crown of thorns

The first *Euphorbia* we shall deal with was also the first to become known as a house plant. It is now considered a little old-fashioned and is rarely found in a modern interior. Perhaps the shape does not fit in; it is, however, extremely hardy and with reasonable care can spread enormously. Sometimes the leaves suddenly drop; when this happens, give the plant a month's rest (very little water) and do not increase moisture until new leaves appear. It can be propagated from cuttings; allow the poisonous juice to dry before inserting them in sandy soil.

☼ Prefers full sun

🌡 Warm (16–20°C (61–68°F) at night); tolerates normal room temperature even in winter

💧 Water very sparingly

💦 Sensitive to excess humidity; ideal for dry living-room atmosphere

🪣 A sandy, slightly chalky mixture

Euphorbia pulcherrima

Poinsettia

The Poinsettia has supplanted the Christmas rose (a Hellebore species) as a Christmas plant. The new strains have very large bracts (the flowers themselves are insignificant), which may keep their colour for over six months. Try to find other colours as well in addition to the red forms.

It is not all that easy to keep the poinsettia after flowering. Try putting it out of doors in summer, and towards the autumn reduce the light supply to ten hours a day, since otherwise it will not flower, and consequently will not produce the coloured bracts either. It is really an expert's job. Propagation is from cuttings taken in summer.

☼ Plenty of light, but out of the sun

🌡 Moderate (10–16°C (50–61°F) at night) to warm (16–20°C (61–68°F) at night). During flowering keep a little cooler

💧 In the flowering season water fairly freely, using tepid water; afterwards water sparingly

💦 Moderate humidity; spray from time to time

🪣 Slightly chalky mixture

Euphorbia

Succulent species

The *Euphorbia* genus is an extremely versatile one; just look at the *Euphorbia meloformis* (left) which looks exactly like a cactus. Only its inflorescence indicates its relationship to, e.g., the poinsettia.

The *Euphorbia pseudocactus* on the right in the photograph, another succulent species, is still quite small: at a later stage it will branch. Large specimens (imported ones are sometimes several metres in height) not only have great decorative value but are also very hardy in indoor cultivation. Their only requirements are little water and, if possible, a cool position in winter.

☼ Well-lit, sunny position; some may be placed out of doors in summer

🌡 Warm (16–20°C (61–68°F) at night); keep cool in winter, like cacti

◊ Water sparingly

〰 Satisfied with low humidity

▼ Sandy/loamy potting mixture

Exacum

In summer this member of the Gentian family is frequently found in well-stocked flower-shops. *Exacum affine* is an annual, sown by the grower from December onwards. The seedlings are pricked out twice and are then planted in threes in 10cm (4in) pots. Flowering commences in June. To make them last do not keep the plants in too warm a position. If you are prepared to spend a little more money, try buying several to fill an antique container or a jardinière.

It is practically impossible to keep the plants after flowering; the result will in any case be unsatisfactory.

☼ Good light, but out of the sun

🌡 Warm (16–20°C (61–68°F) at night)

◊ Water moderately, but make sure the soil-ball does not dry out

〰 Normal living-room atmosphere is adequately humid

▼ Standard potting compost, preferably with a little extra humus

× Fatshedera

In 1912 the Nantes (France) nursery of Lizé-Frères achieved a successful crossing of two genera: *Fatsia japonica* and *Hedera helix*, resulting in × *Fatshedera lizei*. The 'Variegata' strain has cream-mottled foliage. *Fatshedera lizei* itself (illustrated) is all green. In both the leaves are five-lobed.

This semi-climber can grow very tall, and to achieve bushy growth it is necessary to remove the tips several times. The cuttings thus obtained will strike readily either in water or in equal parts of sand and peat fibre in bottom heat; 10cm (4in) sections of stem (with leaves) may also be used. Once the cuttings have rooted, place them in threes in a pot. After a few years they may produce small pale green flowers in the autumn.

× *Fatshedera* is an easy plant, rarely subject to disease. It is important to give the plant a cool position, since otherwise the lower leaves will soon drop. 'Variegata' accepts a slightly higher temperature. The leaves will also almost inevitably drop if after watering the plant is left in a footbath. In winter keep in fairly good light, but out of the sun. If the plant remains in your living-room, it should be regularly sprayed to avoid damage caused by dry air. The leaves should also be sponged from time to time, for otherwise a dust layer will prevent assimilation. × *Fatshedera* should preferably be fed once a fortnight.

To use the plant as ground cover, 30–40cm (12–16in) shoots should be bent down and anchored; they will soon root. It is further worth mentioning that ivy may be grafted on × *Fatshedera* to improve the strain. This applied particularly to variegated forms.

Satisfied with little light, but will also thrive in a better lit spot

Cold (3–10°C (37–50°F) at night), or moderate (10–16°C (50–61°F) at night); may spend the winter in the living-room

Water freely in summer, moderately in winter

If left in the living-room in winter, provide adequate humidity

Standard to chalky potting compost

Fatsia

Castor oil plant

Fatsia japonica, a native of Japan, may grow to as much as 5m (16ft). It does not readily branch; its leaves are 7- to 9-lobed, large and shiny. Older plants may produce small creamy flowers, followed by black berries. Variegated forms such as 'Variegata' and 'Albomarginata' grow a little more slowly than the green strains and require a higher temperature, as much as 14–16°C (57–61°F) in winter. Yellowing leaves indicate too warm and dry an environment. If the plant loses its lower leaves it may be air-layered.

Propagation is from cuttings or from seed. From late winter until August feed weekly.

☼ Requires controlled daylight; tolerates shade; may be placed out of doors in summer

🌡 Cold (3–10°C (37–50°F) at night); variegated strains require a higher temperature than green forms; temperature in winter (6–10°C (43–50°F))

💧 Water freely in the growing season, less thereafter

🌫 Moderate humidity

🪴 Somewhat loamy soil, rich in humus

Faucaria

Tiger's chaps

Of the more than thirty-five succulents belonging to this genus, originating in South Africa, those in cultivation in this country include *Faucaria tigrina*, *Faucaria felina* and *Faucaria lupina*.

The keel-shaped dentate leaves, growing opposite in pairs, are joined at the base. The golden-yellow flowers appear from the end of August onwards. The plants should be re-potted once every three years, in April; they may be divided at the same time. Seed may be sown in spring and cuttings taken from June to August; leave these to dry for two days.

☼ Sunny spot desirable; in summer the plant likes to be placed out of doors

🌡 Moderate (10–16°C (50–61°F) at night); 5°C (41°F) in winter

💧 Water moderately in summer; keep completely dry during the dormant season

🌫 Dry air very well tolerated

🪴 Somewhat loamy, friable mixture

Felicia

Blue daisy

This delightful plant with its sky-blue flowers is rarely cultivated, although it is no less attractive than other annuals, such as *Exacum* or *Torenia*. Seed is easily obtainable; it should be sown from late January onwards in bowls at a temperature of about 16°C (61°F), under glass. Prick out the seedlings and keep fairly cool thereafter. Flowering may continue throughout the year. Between June and August cuttings can be taken from tip-shoots. Plants grown by this method must be kept cool in winter and re-potted in spring.

The photograph shows *Felicia amelloides*.

☼ Requires a well-lit, sunny spot; ensure adequate ventilation

🌡 Moderate (10–16°C (50–61°F) at night)

💧 Water moderately; the soil-ball must be kept constantly moist

💨 Moderate humidity

🪣 Somewhat chalky potting compost

Ferocactus

These barrel-shaped cacti are known for their beautiful spines. The dish contains, from left to right: *F. viridescens*, *F. horridus* and *F. latispinus*. Bright sunshine is essential to achieve fine colouring of the spines; the cacti must therefore be grown near a south-facing window or in a greenhouse. Allow the soil to dry out between watering and use soft water (or rainwater). The pots should be well-drained and not too small. Towards the end of October it is better to stop watering and to turn off the heating, unless the outside temperature is below 5°C (41°F). Resume watering in March, first re-potting the plants.

☼ In summer out of doors in a warm spot in the sun; cool in winter

🌡 Moderate (10–16°C (50–61°F) at night); temperature in winter approx. 8°C (46°F)

💧 Normally in summer; do not water in winter

💨 Low humidity; spray on very hot summer days

🪣 Special cactus mixture

Ficus

Rubber plant

The *Ficus* genus comprises over nine hundred species of immense variety: trees, shrubs, climbing and hanging plants, epiphytes, species that are winter-hardy and others that are not, deciduous and evergreen forms, etc. The species used as house plants originate in Southern and South-Eastern Asia (especially in India and Indonesia), Australia and various parts of Africa. The fig-tree, *Ficus carica*, is indigenous in Southern Europe and in North Africa.

In spite of this variety there is, of course, some botanical affinity. This may be found, for instance, in the unusual inflorescence and the fruits: the extremely insignificant flowers are found in spherical to pear-shaped stem sections, which later develop into fig-shaped fruits. Another common characteristic is the milky secretion; in some *Ficus* species this was once of commercial importance. Today other species are used for the production of latex, so that the *Ficus* is now of ornamental value only.

The *Ficus benjamina* in the upper photograph has a graceful appearance because of the curving twigs and leaves which make it look a little like a weeping willow. This *Ficus* grows very rapidly without requiring too much light, and in the course of a few years may hit the ceiling.

Ficus deltoidea (lower photograph) is the only species to produce fruit in the living-room; it does so already at an early age. The pseudo-fruits are yellowish-green, round and 1cm ($\frac{2}{5}$in) in diameter. As a rule this plant remains fairly small; it has oval leaves, pointed at the lower end, and is reasonably freely branching. A fairly high degree of humidity must be maintained. The fact that the *Ficus* is such an easy and widely-grown plant is due mainly to its leathery foliage, which reduces evaporation. A dry, warm atmosphere is there-

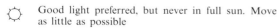

☼ Good light preferred, but never in full sun. Move as little as possible

🌡 Warm (16–20°C (61–68°F) at night); in the dormant season the temperature must not drop below 12°C (54°F)

💧 Fairly freely in the growing season; the soil-ball must not be allowed to dry out. Water sparingly in winter

Spray regularly

Slightly chalky mixture

Ficus (continued)

fore tolerated. Nevertheless the foliage, particularly when variegated, should be sprayed or sponged to remove dust.

It is advisable always to give tepid water. In winter the soil should only just be kept moist. In the growing season feed every fortnight.

A proprietary potting compost is satisfactory, but an even better mixture can be composed from leafmould, rotted turves, peat fibre and sand. Adequate drainage is most important; water should never be allowed to collect at the bottom of the pot. To grow the plant from cuttings a propagator is really essential, for only a bottom temperature of 25–30°C (77–86°F) will give a reasonable chance of success. Frequently eye cuttings are used; cut the stem 1cm ($\frac{2}{5}$in) above and below an eye; this will give you a cutting with an eye, a leaf-stem and a leaf. In large-leaved species, such as *Ficus elastica*, the leaf is rolled up and held in position with a rubber band in order to minimise evaporation. The cuttings are grown in equal parts of sand and peat, thoroughly moistened and placed in a well-lit spot, but not in full sun. When they have rooted, the little plants are gradually hardened off and potted as soon as the first leaf appears. Plants may also be grown from seed or by air-layering, a method for which *Ficus elastica* provides a textbook example. It is used chiefly to induce the plant to branch, or when it has lost its lower leaves.

The well-known *Ficus elastica* 'Decora', a product of specific seed selection, grows upwards until the ceiling gets in the way or until you prune the top. The variety shown in the upper photograph is one of the finest variegated forms available. Remember that 'Decora' is sensitive to temperature variations, too warm an environment in winter and too low a soil temperature.

The *Ficus lyrata* (syn. *Ficus pandurata*) has enormous, violin-shaped waxy leaves with a wavy edge. It is best used as a specimen plant, lit from all sides. Other erect growing species are: *Ficus bengalensis*, which has large leaves, hairy especially on the reverse and in young plants, may grow to a great height, and has aerial roots; and *Ficus cyathistipula*, which has pale green leaves, up to 20cm (8in) in length, and is freely branching. Temperature 14–20°C

Ficus (continued)

(57–68°F).

Ficus aspera (syn. *Ficus parcelli*) is a hot-house plant—a small shrub with large white-and-green marbled foliage; at a fairly early age it produces cherry-like red-and-white veined figs. The temperature should never drop below 20°C (68°F).

Ficus religiosa requires plenty of light and air. The leaves are thin, long-stalked and up to 15cm (6in) in length. *Ficus retusa* is a dense shrub, whose branches, at first growing erect, will subsequently droop. *Ficus rubiginosa* is a plant for an unheated greenhouse (winter temperature 10–12°C (50–54°F); may be placed in a sheltered outdoor position in summer), with blunt, shiny green and leathery leaves, up to 10cm (4in) in length. There is a variegated form, 'Variegata'. The twigs will root easily.

A well-known recumbent or climbing form is called *Ficus pumila* (upper photograph), with small, heart-shaped leaves; it is very suitable for being trained up a wall in place of ivy and within a short time may cover a considerable area. *Ficus radicans*, a creeper, has 5–10cm (2–4in) long leaves. Roots are developed from the leaf-buds; it is fabulous as groundcover in plant troughs. The plant in the lower photograph is the variegated form 'Variegata'.

A less well-known species is *Ficus montana*, whose leaves resemble oakleaves; at one time it was occasionally referred to as *Ficus quercifolia*. It is suitable as a hanging plant.

Other photographs of *Ficus* plant may be found in the introductory chapters of this book. If they are properly cared for, the chance of disease is slight. Since these fast-growing plants naturally require a great deal of nourishment, timely re-potting is essential. Often they are kept in tiny pots until they capsize; this, of course, is asking for trouble. Feeding is not enough, for in the long run the soil will be poisoned by the minerals it retains.

☼ Good light preferred, but never in full sun

🌡 Warm (16–20°C (61–68°F) at night); in the resting period the temperature must not drop below 12°C (54°F)

💧 Fairly freely in the growing season; never let the soil-ball dry out. Sparingly in winter

💦 Spray regularly

🪴 Slightly chalky mixture

Fittonia

These beautiful foliage plants will thrive only in a high degree of humidity. Kept on the windowsill in ordinary flower-pots they will droop, but in a well filled container, in a plant window, or even in a shallow bowl, they will do better.

The foliage should be frequently sprayed. The soil must be very friable and constantly. moist. Flowering plants demonstrate their relationship to *Aphelandra*. The photograph shows two forms of *Fittonia verschaffeltii*, namely 'Pearcei' (foreground) and 'Argyroneura'. Propagation is from cuttings in spring, warm and under glass.

☼ Requires a fair amount of light, but is sensitive to direct sunlight

🌡 Warm (16–20°C (61–68°F) at night)

💧 Water moderately throughout the year, using tepid, soft water

〰 Very high degree of humidity essential

🍶 Friable mixture, rich in humus, e.g. a proprietary potting compost with extra coarse sand

Fuchsia

The finest *Fuchsia* plants are grown in a cool, shady greenhouse, where they can remain throughout the winter at a low temperature. However, many species will thrive on the windowsill, away from the sun, while other strains will do extremely well out of doors. Success depends on finding a suitable spot; you will have to experiment. *Fuchsia* plants respond to the special care which true plant lovers will give them; without such individual care they will never flower very well.

Another very important factor is the correct soil mixture. A *Fuchsia* lover will usually make this up from leafmould, loam, rotted cow manure and some dried blood. However, a proprietary potting compost may be used instead.

For outdoor cultivation plastic pots are preferable to clay pots, since they allow less evaporation.

In the flowering season the plants must frequently be fed.

The lower photograph on the facing page shows the erect-growing small-flowered 'Dollar

Fuchsia (continued)

Princess'; on this page you see the hanging form 'La Campanella', which has larger flowers.

Fuchsia plants are easily grown from cuttings. They must on no account be kept in too warm an environment. To achieve bushy growth the tips should repeatedly be pinched out; by continuing this process flowering may be delayed. Special pruning will result in pyramid-shaped or standard plants; these are at their best in the second or third year. Thousands of strains are available from specialist growers.

☼ Half-shady position in summer; plenty of light, but no direct sunlight in winter

🌡 Moderate (10–16°C (50–61°F) at night); 10°C (50°F) in winter

💧 Maintain constant moisture; in winter water a little more sparingly than in summer

💨 Try to maintain a fairly high degree of humidity to avoid the buds dropping

🪣 Use slightly chalky soil

Gardenia

Cape jasmine

In the United States and the British Isles gardenias are still used as buttonholes; on the continent of Europe the custom appears to have died out. As a house plant, too, *Gardenia jasminioides* is most attractive and the deliciously scented flowers are a cheerful sight in spring. Make sure that the atmosphere is not too dry; grow the plant throughout the year near a well lit window, keeping it warm in winter as well.

In January young shoots may be rooted in bottom heat. The plants may also be grown from seed. Do not feed after the beginning of August.

☼ Plenty of light, but screen from direct sunlight. May be put out of doors in summer

🌡 Warm (16–20°C (61–68°F) at night); 16–18°C (61–64°F) in winter; soil temperature must be maintained at a minimum of 18°C (64°F)

💧 Water moderately, using tepid, soft water

💨 Frequently spray the foliage

🪣 Potting compost rich in humus

Gasteria

These succulents are very similar to *Haworthia* (see p. 98), but they are somewhat more robust in habit. The leaves are sword-shaped, fleshy and often covered in pearly warts or grey blotches.

In summer these strong plants may be put out of doors, and even in the sun, without disaster. They do not need much water; this would in fact be fatal in winter, when they must be placed in a cool spot. Red, orange or pink flowers appear at the tip of tall stems, particularly if the plants have been allowed a resting period. Propagation is from leaf cuttings or from seed.

The species illustrated is *Gasteria verrucosa*.

☼ Puts up with either a sunny position or light shade

🌡 Warm (16–20°C (61–68°F) at night), cooler in winter (6–12°C (43–54°F))

◊ Water very moderately, especially in the cooler season

〰 Extremely well suited to a dry atmosphere

🍶 Friable, chalky mixture

Grevillea

Silk bark oak

In Queensland and New South Wales (Australia) this plant grows into a tree of up to 20m (65ft). It resembles a fern but is nothing of the sort. Young specimens that are repeatedly topped may occasionally branch more freely, which improves their appearance, but as a rule *Grevillea robusta* spreads little. This plant is happiest in a cool stair-well or a fairly well lit corridor. It is most inadvisable to combine it with other plants in a warm room. Propagation is from imported seed; plant out in good time in nutritious soil, 3–5 to a pot; cover the drainage hole with a good-sized crock.

☼ Semi-shade in summer, good light in winter

🌡 Moderate (10–16°C (50–61°F) at night); prefers to spend the winter in a cool spot (4–8°C (39–46°F))

◊ Water moderately; the soil-ball must not dry out

〰 Spray frequently, especially in spring when the plant puts forth new shoots

🍶 Chalky soil mixture

Guzmania

These are little known but attractive bromeliads, sometimes used in combination with
other plants in troughs or for other decorative
purposes. In these circumstances it matters
little whether or not the growing conditions
are ideal, for the flowering rosettes are already
dying; this process can be delayed, but not
halted, by cooling the environment. The guide-
lines below therefore apply chiefly to the
plant's propagation from the offsets forming at
the base of the rosette; these should not be
removed until the mother plant has faded. The
young plants are not easy to grow in the living-
room. The form illustrated is *Guzmania lingu-
lata* 'Minor'.

☼   A plant for a semi-shady spot

🌡   Warm (16–20°C (61–68°F) at night); minimum temperature in winter 16°C (61°F)

💧   Give tepid, soft water, poured into the funnel in
summer only; in winter keep drier

   Spray frequently in summer; never in winter

🪣   Acid, friable soil

Gymnocalycium

These are unusually coloured little cacti,
always grafted on a green stem to survive. The
red globes are not flowers, although flowers
may appear in due course, as shown by the
specimen in the centre of the photograph.
From left to right you see the *Gymnocalycium
mihanovichii* strains 'Rosea', 'Black Cap' and
'Optima Rubra'. A yellow mutation is also
available. The plants freely produce offsets (see
the centre plant); these may be removed and
grafted separately. Both the base and the
globular offset are cut level; they need only
be pressed together and temporarily secured.

☼   Good light, but sensitive to direct sunlight

🌡   Moderate (10–16°C (50–61°F) at night) to warm
(16–20°C (61–68°F) at night); in winter about 10°C
(50°F)

💧   Water very sparingly; keep dry in winter

   Dry living-room atmosphere adequate

🪣   Friable, chalky potting compost or special cactus
mixture

95

Gynura

The decorative value of these little plants lies chiefly in their fine, velvety foliage with its purple sheen, which shows to best advantage in good light. The yellow flowers produced by mature plants have an unpleasant smell and therefore do not add to their attraction. You would do best perpetually to take cuttings; these strike very easily and you will thus always have fresh young plants. Do not spray the foliage—this will cause staining.

In winter the *Gynura aurantiaca* illustrated in the upper photograph will become unsightly as a result of inadequate light, although it will usually survive.

☼ To maintain the purple sheen the plant must have plenty of light, but keep it out of the sun

🌡 Warm (16–20°C (61–68°F) at night)

💧 Water freely in the growing period (not on the leaves); moderately in winter

🌫 Moderate humidity

🪴 Standard proprietary potting compost

Habranthus

A little known bulbous plant, obtainable from mail-order firms, this is treated in approximately the same way as the familiar amaryllis or *Hippeastrum*. This means that in the autumn it is placed in well-draining pots, preferably about 5 to a pot. At first keep fairly cool, at about 10–15°C (50–59°F) and give hardly any water. When the bulbs put forth shoots keep a little warmer and moister. After flowering the foliage will continue to grow for a time; afterwards keep the soil increasingly dry until all the leaves have faded. Re-pot only once every 2 or 3 years.

The photograph shows *Habranthus robustus*.

☼ Not in full sun, but requires plenty of light

🌡 Moderate (10–16°C (50–61°F) at night); after flowering allow a resting period

💧 Water moderately

🌫 Moderate humidity

🪴 Nutritious mixture, rich in humus

Haemanthus

Blood lily

The bulbs or young plants of various Blood lily species are obtainable from mail-order firms; they are rarely found at the florist. The plants are despatched in spring and on receipt they are potted in nutritious soil. Water sparingly at first, a little more when the shoot develops. At the end of the summer the plant should be allowed to die back by withholding water.

The species *Haemanthus albiflos*, which is evergreen and is therefore despatched in leaf, requires different treatment; this clivia-like plant is placed in a slightly cooler position in winter, but must be watered throughout the year. It dislikes being transplanted and consequently often loses its foliage, but new leaves will appear in due course. It is a very hardy house plant. Red-flowered species are more difficult to cultivate; they require bottom heat and are best grown in a greenhouse.

Haemanthus albiflos has elongated smooth and fleshy leaves and white flowers with long stamens and yellow anthers.

Haemanthus katharinae dies back in winter; it has 4–5 leaves on a short stem. The flowers are red and very large, up to 24cm (9$\frac{1}{2}$in) across.

Haemanthus multiflorus (illustrated) resembles the last species in treatment as well as in appearance, but the flowers are smaller. It flowers in April; the leaves develop later. The plant must continue to be properly cared for as otherwise it will not flower in the following year.

It is not necessary to re-pot every year; in many cases it is sufficient to replace the top layer by fresh soil and to re-pot in the second or third year.

New plants may be grown from offsets, but it will take several years (in a greenhouse) before the young plants can flower.

A sunny situation; the plant dislikes being moved

Warm (16–20°C (61–68°F) at night); slightly cooler in winter (12–15°C (54–59°F))

Water normally; less from mid-August onwards; keep practically dry in winter to give the plant a rest

Fairly high degree of humidity desirable

Potting soil rich in humus

Hamatocactus

These freely flowering cacti are relatively easy to grow and are often found in a cactus-lover's greenhouse. They can be grown on the windowsill as well, provided they are given a cool spot during the winter resting period. Several species are in cultivation; they are conspicuous because of the large curved central spines. The *Hamatocactus setispinus* illustrated is probably the best known species; it has 12–14 ribs and fragrant yellow flowers with a red throat. Even young plants may flower profusely. It should be preferably grown in plastic pots to reduce drying of the soil-ball.

Propagation is from seed.

☼ Plenty of sun

🌡 Moderate (10–16°C (50–61°F) at night) to warm (16–20°C (61–68°F) at night); cool in winter

💧 Water sparingly; keep drier in winter

💨 Low humidity is desirable

🪣 Friable, chalky mixture or special cactus mixture

Haworthia

This genus of succulents belongs to the Lily family. Most species originate in the Cape Province; they possess thick fleshy leaves, arranged in rosettes. Offsets are frequently produced at the base. New plants are grown from these offsets or from seed. The dormant season of *Haworthia* species with transparent foliage is from June to September; plants with pearly warts on the reverse of the leaves, such as the *H. reinwardtii* illustrated should have a resting season from October to February at a temperature of 10–12°C (50–54°F). Other well-known species with pearl-covered leaves are *H. attenuata*, *H. fasciata*, *H. margaritifera* and *H. papillosa*.

☼ Very well-lit position; the plant does not like direct sunlight

🌡 Warm (16–20°C (61–68°F) at night); in the dormant season 5–16°C (41–61°F) depending on the species

💧 Water moderately (no water among the leaves); very sparingly in the dormant season

💨 No special requirements

🪣 Slightly chalky mixture

Hebe

The *Hebe andersonii* hybrid illustrated is an evergreen shrubby plant with small leathery leaves.
It flowers in late summer and in the autumn.
The plant in the photograph has purple
racemes, but there are white- and red-flowered
forms as well. In many cases the flowers drop
when the temperature in the living-room is too
high and the air too dry. After flowering the
plants must be cut back. The cuttings may be
rooted in moderate bottom heat. In the growing season give a small feed every week. In
winter keep at 6–10°C (43–50°F), in contrast
to a number of garden species which will tolerate temperatures as low as −20°C (−4°F). The
plant is often called *Veronica*.

☼ In summer a sheltered outdoor position; bring indoors in good time, for the plant is very sensitive
to cold

🌡 Moderate to cool (5–12°C (41–54°F)

💧 Water freely in summer, sparingly in winter

⋰ Moderate humidity

🪴 Standard proprietary potting compost or a chalky
mixture rich in humus

Hedera

Ivy

These well-known house plants definitely
require a cool environment. Propagation from
cuttings is very easy, especially in the autumn.
The common garden species can also be grown
indoors, but as a rule small-leaved decorative
forms of *Hedera helix* are used for this purpose; for instance, 'Garland' (foreground left
in the photograph) and 'Glacier' (centre). There
are numerous other strains, but not all are winter-hardy. The sub-species *canariensis* is
another ivy which is not hardy; this is usually
available in the variegated form 'Variegata',
sometimes called 'Gloire de Marengo' (photograph, right). It tolerates a slightly higher temperature.

☼ Is satisfied with little light

🌡 Cool to moderate (4–12°C (39–54°F) at night); in
winter an unheated but frostfree room

💧 Water moderately; the soil-ball must remain moist;
in winter water sparingly

⋰ Spray frequently in summer; sponge the leaves from
time to time

🪴 Somewhat chalky soil

99

Hemigraphis

These are relatively unknown tropical foliage plants requiring a high degree of humidity. In Malaysia they are often grown in gardens; we use them chiefly as groundcover in greenhouses, although occasionally they keep in remarkably good condition in indoor plant combinations. Usually *Hemigraphis alternata* (illustrated) is used for this purpose; its leaves have a beautiful silvery-purple sheen. In a heated indoor propagator young tip-shoots will easily root at any time of the year. Pinch out the tips from the young plants once or twice to encourage branching.

 A shadow plant; never place in full sun

 Warm (16–20°C (61–68°F) at night)

 Water moderately with demineralised water

 Requires a high degree of humidity and is therefore difficult to keep in the living-room

Somewhat chalky mixture

Hibiscus

Chinese rose

This freely flowering shrub, an ornament to numerous gardens in the tropics and subtropics, has become a popular house plant. Whereas at one time only the single red form was cultivated, it is now mainly the double, yellow, copper-coloured and salmon-pink strains that are found on the market.

Nevertheless, the single red strain (with flowers similar to those of the variegated 'Cooperi' illustrated on the facing page) was much more satisfactory in cultivation. Some people owned shrubs a metre in diameter, with innumerable flowers, something never seen in double-flowered strains. However, the common *Hibiscus* is not easily obtainable. You might be lucky and get hold of a cutting. These plants should initially be kept warm. A resting period in winter in a fairly cool position remains essential for successful cultivation. At this time the plants may be cut back quite drastically. Take care that the soil does not dry out too much, for this will kill the Chinese rose.

Hibiscus (continued)

The photograph on the preceding page shows a well-known double form of *Hibiscus rosa-sinensis*. On this page you see the variegated 'Cooperi', which is chiefly used as a foliage plant, but nevertheless produces a flower from time to time. All strains tolerate full sun, but the variegated form requires extra good ventilation as well.

From early June onwards the plants may be placed out of doors, but only in a very sheltered position. The single red form is most suited to this purpose.

Propagation is only from cuttings in bottom heat, under glass or plastic.

☼ Likes a sunny position; in summer it may be placed in a sheltered outdoor spot

🌡 Warm (16–20°C (61–68°F) at night); 12–15°C (54–59°F) during the dormant season in winter

◊ Requires a regular and generous water supply, but a little less in winter

⚘ Occasional spraying advisable

🝪 Chalky soil, rich in humus

Hippeastrum

Amaryllis

As a rule the *Hippeastrum*, often called amaryllis, is brought into flower very successfully; not surprising, therefore, that these bulbs are so popular. I should like to point out that named strains, though a little more expensive, have flowers far more beautiful than those of bulbs sold in the supermarket by colour only. In the photograph you see, from left to right: 'Belinda' (also shown on p. 102), 'Fire Dance' and 'President Tito'. Other fine forms are the so-called 'Picotee' strains with a contrasting margin to the petals.

These named bulbs are obtainable only from specialist growers who will be pleased to supply you by mail order. Usually it is possible to indicate the size of the bulbs required. Extra large bulbs may produce three or four flower stems.

Prepared bulbs may be potted as early as November. Cover the pot with a plastic bag and place in a warm position, possibly even above a radiator, provided it is not too hot.

Hippeastrum (continued)

Make sure the soil-ball does not dry out.

When the flower stem has reached 15–20cm (6–8in) the plant may be placed in a well-lit window where it is to flower. The leaves will not properly start into growth until after flowering. If you want to keep the bulb for another season, the foliage should develop at a minimum temperature of 20°C (68°F). The flower stem is cut off close to the bulb. Water freely and feed once a fortnight. From September onwards gradually decrease watering until the leaves have died, and keep the bulb dry in the pot. In January carefully replace the soil-ball with fresh soil and start into growth once more.

☼   Plenty of light, but screen from bright sunlight

🌡   Moderate (10–16°C (50–61°F) at night); keep the bulb at 6°C (43°F) in winter

💧   Water regularly in the growing and flowering season; from September onwards cease watering

💨   Moderate humidity

🪣   Well-drained loamy soil, rich in humus

Homalocladium

The stems of this remarkable plant, which has reached us from the Solomon Islands, have taken over the function of the foliage. Occasionally leaves are produced as well, but as a rule these quickly drop, as if they find themselves superfluous. Although rare, the plant is easy to grow, since from late May onwards it may be placed out of doors.

In winter the most favourable temperature lies between 8 and 16°C (46–61°F). Cuttings readily strike root in slight heat. Combine a few of the young plants in one pot. Mature plants produce small flowers and pink-purple fruits.

Illustrated is *Homalocladium platycladum*.

☼   Very well-lit or sunny position; may be stood outside in summer

🌡   Warm (16–20°C (61–68°F) at night), but lower temperatures are well tolerated

💧   Water moderately

💨   Spray occasionally; the air should not be too dry

🪣   Loamy mixture rich in humus, or calcareous standard potting compost

Howeia

Kentia palm

Now that the more modern tubs and cylinders are being used for larger house plants, even palms look less 'old-fashioned'. This is indeed fortunate, for their characteristics make them ideal and very adaptable house plants. The resting period in winter means only that feeding should cease. In undrained containers beware of overwatering, for palms are very sensitive to wet feet. When re-planting it is best to use deep pots, well-drained if possible. Propagation is from seed.

The photograph shows *Howeia forsteriana*.

☼ A plant for a shady spot

🌡 Moderate (10–16°C (50–61°F) at night); keep moderately warm in winter (14–18°C (57–64°F))

💧 Water moderately throughout the year, preferably with softened water

🌫 Spray regularly

🪣 Friable soil, rich in humus; must also contain some clay or loam

Hoya bella

Wax flower

This is the more difficult and less striking of the two species of wax flower which can be grown in the living-room. For the purpose of the photograph the tendrils have been tied to supports, as otherwise the pendulous flowers would hardly be visible. A high degree of humidity and temperature are most desirable. Little sun is required. It is best to grow the plants in hanging pots filled with a humusy mixture, so that the flowers are seen from below; these appear in the period May–September. Give the plant cooler and drier conditions in winter to prevent an attack by aphids. Propagation is from cuttings.

☼ Slightly shady position; do not turn the plant

🌡 Warm (minimum 16°C (61°F) at night); minimum in winter 13°C (55°F)

💧 Water moderately; keep a little drier in the dormant season

🌫 High degree of humidity; spray frequently

🪣 Friable, crumbly soil with a lot of peat, in well-draining hanging pots or baskets

Hoya carnosa

Large wax flower

The large wax flower illustrated is an excellent house plant which may last for a long time. The long, winding stems must be trained on bent wire. After the buds appear the plant must not be turned, even though the flowers will always grow on the side facing the window. When they open the flower umbels exude delicious honey. Do not remove the flower-stalks; a second flowering frequently follows. Strains with variegated leaves are fairly rare.

Propagation is possible from cuttings in June–July, rooted in bottom heat and under glass.

☼ Good light, screened from brightest sunlight

🌡 Warm (minimum 16°C (61°F) at night); minimum 10°C (50°F) in winter

💧 Water moderately; a little more in summer; keep drier in the dormant season

💨 Tolerates normal living-room atmosphere, but likes to be sprayed frequently

🪴 Friable, crumbly soil, containing peat, charcoal and rotted cow manure; well-draining

Hyacinthus

Hyacinth

Prepared bulbs may be potted from early October onwards. It is best to bury the pots in a pit, not too dry and protected against frost. If they are placed in a cool dark cellar instead it is advisable to pull plastic bags over the pots. During this rooting period the soil temperature must be kept at 9–13°C (48–55°F). When you can feel that the flower-bud has left the bulb, the pots may be brought into the light. Place them near a cool window.

If you prefer to grow them in water or in gravel, be sure to keep the water a few millimetres below the bulbs. After flowering the bulbs will be worthless.

☼ Good light, but out of full sun; keep in the dark to start them into growth

🌡 The bulbs should be rooted in a cool, frostfree place (8–10 weeks); they must then be kept cool for about 9 days, increasing to 15°C (59°F)

💧 Water moderately with slightly softened water

💨 Moderate humidity

🪴 Sandy, porous soil, not too rich

Hydrangea

Hortensia

Hortensias used to be grown on a much larger scale than is now the case. Nevertheless, there are still devotees for whom it is a real sport to bring the plants into flower season after season. A cool, shady situation is essential to achieve successful results. A hortensia will never be happy in a centrally (over-) heated living-room with windows on all sides. A cool hall, facing east, or even north, is much better. If the foliage droops, immediate plunging may save the plant.

In summer, plenty of water and liquid fertiliser are required. At that time the pot is best buried in the garden, in a slightly shady and airy but not draughty position. Use rainwater whenever possible, for tapwater contains too much lime. Plants with blue flowers, created by the addition of aluminium sulphate or iron to the soil, are particularly sensitive to hard water.

Immediately after flowering the branches are cut back a little; if possible the plant is re-potted in acid soil. From the end of August onwards stop feeding and reduce the water supply. At the onset of frost the plant must be brought indoors, but to prevent the buds dropping it should have a very cool position. Transfer to a slightly warmer situation must be very gradual.

All indoor hortensias are forms of *Hydrangea macrophylla*. They are not entirely winter-hardy, and if you plant them in the garden the buds may freeze in winter. The lower photograph shows an extra hardy garden strain of the same species, growing happily in acid soil among rhododendrons.

New plants are grown from young shoots without a flower-bud; these are rooted in May–July in bottom heat. The cultivation of young plants should really be confined to a cold frame or an unheated greenhouse.

☼　Plenty of light, but definitely out of the sun

🌡　Moderate (10–16°C (50–61°F) at night); temperature in winter 4–8°C (39–46°F)

💧　Freely during the flowering season; in the dormant season the soil-ball must not dry out. Soft water

〰　Moderate humidity

🪴　Friable, peaty soil, rich in humus

Hypocyrta

This accommodating plant with its unusually shaped flowers deserves a place in the living-room or the greenhouse. The best known species is *Hypocyrta glabra* (illustrated), which has small shiny dark green leaves on erect growing or curving stems. The rotund orange flowers emerge from the axils. A low temperature in winter is essential for bud formation; so is bright sunshine. Prune before the plant starts into new growth, for *Hypocyrta* flowers on the new shoots.

Propagation is from cuttings, which root easily even in ordinary potting soil; 6–8 cuttings to a pot will produce a bushy plant.

Likes slight shade, but some sun is essential to ensure flowering

Warm (16–20°C (61–68°F) at night; in winter keep at 12°C (54°F)

Water moderately; avoid excessive watering especially during the resting period

High degree of humidity in the growing season is excellent

Mixture of leafmould, sphagnum and charcoal

Hypoestes

Hypoestes taeniata is a native of Madagascar; it owes its beauty chiefly to its mottled foliage. The small, labiate flowers, usually lilac in colour, are very inconspicuous.

This plant may grow profusely, particularly in a heated greenhouse. If it spreads too much, or if it loses its lower leaves, it should be drastically cut back. It is easily grown from cuttings, especially in spring in a greenhouse, in bottom heat. Pinching out the tips will produce a bushy plant; all the tip shoots can be used as cuttings. These are best rooted in shallow bowls; the soil should not be firmed too much. New plants may also be grown successfully from seed.

Slight shade; likes fresh air

Warm (16–20°C (61–68°F) at night

Water fairly freely in the growing season, using lukewarm soft water

Ensure a high degree of humidity, especially in summer, and spray very frequently

Slightly acid soil, rich in humus

Impatiens

Busy Lizzie

The *Impatiens balsamina* illustrated in the upper photograph has pale green foliage and double pink flowers; it is very suitable for use on the balcony or in the garden. The lower photograph shows *Impatiens walleriana*, a fairly low-growing species for pot cultivation. The spurred flowers range in colour from deep red to white; the foliage is bright green. The decorative form 'Petersiana' has bronze-coloured to red stems and leaves, and red flowers.

The above are the most commonly domesticated species, but the mountains of tropical eastern Africa have yielded others of the same genus; for instance, *Impatiens repens*, with small, dark green leaves on creeping stems and large yellow flowers; and *Impatiens niamniamensis*, an erect growing species with unusual red flowers and fairly large green leaves on unbranched stems.

Propagation is child's play: cuttings will readily strike both in water and in sharp sand. The Latin word *impatiens* means 'unable to endure'; this refers to the fact that the seed capsules open to the touch. The seed will germinate in about 10 days.

Young plants should have their tips pinched out several times to encourage branching. Pot in a friable but nutritious mixture. Feed weekly in the growing season.

If the leaves drop, the cause may usually be found in too low a temperature. In too dark a position the flowers will drop. Rotting stems can be due only to constant overwatering. If the plant has grown lanky, it is advisable to take cuttings and grow new specimens.

Excessively dry air may result in whitefly or greenfly. Do not spray when the plant is in flower, for this will cause staining. Red spider may occur if the plant stands in the sun.

☼ Well-lit position, but out of the sun; half-shady in the autumn and in spring

🌡 Moderate (10–16°C (61–68°F) at night); the plants will continue to flower in a winter temperature of 13°C (55°F)

💧 Always water freely, using soft water, except in a resting period

💨 Moderate humidity

🪣 Friable potting mixture, rich in humus

Ipomoea

Morning glory

This attractive climber is very easily grown from seed. Soak the seed for 24 hours, or make scratches on the individual seeds to aid rapid germination; then sow at 18°C (64°F). The *Ipomoea violacea* illustrated has soft green, heart-shaped leaves and large, funnel-shaped flowers, white at the centre, merging into deep blue. A very suitable house plant is *Ipomoea learii*, which produces a profusion of blue flowers. It is of spreading habit and a large tub is needed to accommodate the root system. The plant may be pruned at any time.

 This plant requires as much sun as you can give it

 Warm (16–20°C (61–68°F) at night)

 Water freely, especially in warm and sunny periods, using tepid water

 Spray frequently, again with tepid water

 Standard potting compost or a slightly chalky mixture

Iresine

Iresine herbstii is a shrub-like annual with red stems. The surface of the leaves is reddish-brown and slightly ruffled, crimson along the veins. The decorative form 'Aureireticulata' has gold-mottled foliage and red stems with centre veins. Another all red species is *Iresine lindenii*; this has smooth pointed leaves and is of more bushy habit than *Iresine herbstii*.

   Tip cuttings root easily. To achieve a shapely plant the tips should be nipped out several times. In summer the plant may be placed out of doors. The striking red colour is caused by the pigment anthocyanin.

 A sunny position

 Moderate (10–16°C (50–61°F) at night) to warm (16–20°C (61–68°F) at night)

 Give plenty of tepid water; make sure the soil-ball does not dry out

 Moderate humidity

 Somewhat chalky mixture

Ixora

This genus comprises over two hundred ever-green shrubs and trees, of which the *Ixora coccinea* hybrids are the best known house plants. 'Bier's Glory' (illustrated) has orange-red flowers which may appear at any time from May to September. After flowering the plant is cut back to achieve more compact growth and more profuse flowering in the following year. At this time reduce the water supply to give the plant a short rest. If necessary re-pot in a friable mixture containing leafmould. Tip cuttings are rooted in spring in bottom heat at 25°C (77°F). Pinch out the tips after the appearance of every second pair of leaves. Mature plants may flower three times a year.

☼	Slight shade; do not move and keep out of the sun
🌡	Warm (16–20°C (61–68°F) at night); minimum temperature in winter 16°C (61°F); bottom temperature about 19°C (66°F)
💧	Water normally in the growing season, using soft water; in winter give a little less water
〰	Maintain a high degree of humidity
🏺	Potting mixture rich in humus

Jacaranda

In its native Brazil the *Jacaranda* grows into a tree with graceful foliage and a profusion of lilac flowers.

Jacaranda mimosifolia is popular as a house plant chiefly because of its beautiful feathery foliage.

Propagation from seed at about 25°C (77°F), or from cuttings in spring or summer; half-ripe shoots are used for this purpose. In the growing season give a lime-free liquid feed every second week.

In the course of time the lower leaves will probably drop. When the plant has reached 50–60cm (20–24in) it may have its tip removed from time to time.

☼	Plenty of light and space; possibly some diffused sunlight
🌡	Warm (16–20°C (61–68°F) at night); minimum temperature in winter 14°C (57°F)
💧	Do not overwater (use soft water!); keep even drier in winter
〰	A humid atmosphere is essential
🏺	Lime-free mixture

Jacobinia carnea

Jacobinia species suitable for indoor cultivation may be divided into two groups as regards appearance and treatment. *Jacobinia carnea* (see photograph) and *Jacobinia pohliana* have a terminal inflorescence consisting of slender, tubular pink flowers; in the case of *Jacobinia carnea* this is sticky. The leaves are soft and hairy. Cuttings are rooted from January to April in bottom heat. Mature plants are cut back after flowering (August–September) and are then placed in a well ventilated, moderately heated greenhouse at 12–16°C (54–61°F). The plants are kept at 12–14°C (54–57°F) in winter. In spring they are re-potted into roomy pots; the tips should be nipped out 2–3 times.

- ☼ Roomy spot in slight shade preferred; ventilate often
- 🌡 Warm (16–20°C (61–68°F) at night); temperature in winter 10–14°C (50–57°F), rising to 21°C (70°F) in early spring
- 💧 Maintain constant moisture
- ⛆ Fairly high degree of humidity in summer; not too dry in winter
- 🪴 Slightly chalky, nutritious potting compost

Jacobinia pauciflora

Together with *Jacobinia ghiesbreghtiana* and *Jacobinia* × *penrhosiensis*, *Jacobinia pauciflora* (lower photograph) belongs to the winter-flowering group, with leathery leaves and scattered flowers or small plumes. The flowers of *Jacobinia pauciflora* are red and yellow and are placed in the axils of the leaves. These species are very sensitive to drying of the soil-ball, which will immediately cause them to shed their leaves. Propagation is from cuttings in bottom heat, in January–February. Keep fairly warm at first until, after re-potting, the root system has developed. The plant should then be given a slightly cooler position; the tips should be pinched out once or twice.

- ☼ Requires more sun than *Jacobinia carnea*; may be placed out of doors in summer
- 🌡 A little cooler (12–18°C (54–64°F) at night); as low as 6–10°C (43–50°F) until the flowers appear
- 💧 Never let the soil-ball dry out
- ⛆ Maintain a high degree of humidity, especially in the flowering season, spray occasionally
- 🪴 Slightly chalky potting compost, rich in humus

Jasminum

Jasmine

The abundantly flowering plant in the photograph is *Jasminum officinale*, a native of China. The deliciously scented flowers appear in sparse clusters from early summer until the autumn. After flowering the plant is drastically pruned. To bring it into flower again a greenhouse is almost indispensable, for the jasmine requires a high degree of humidity and plenty of light. From May until September it is placed out of doors in full sun. New plants may be grown by layering or from half-ripe cuttings.

☼ The best possible light in the living-room, but not in full sun; out of doors in summer

🌡 Moderate (10–16°C (50–61°F) at night); keep cool in winter: minimum temperature about 2°C (36°F)

💧 Constant water supply, fairly generous in the growing period

💨 Frequent spraying is excellent

🪴 Porous, slightly chalky potting compost

Kalanchoe

Among the more than two hundred species of this genus of succulents, most of which originate in Africa and Madagascar, *Kalanchoe Blossfeldiana* (illustrated) is the best known form. Like all *Kalanchoe* species it is a typical short-day plant which may be brought into flower at any time of the year by artificial daylight control. The choice is constantly growing: there are strains with yellow, orange, red and pink flower umbels, growing to varying heights. They are grown under glass from seed or from cuttings. The plants like plenty of light and fresh air. Too much sunlight turns the foliage red. In the growing period the plant should be fed every fortnight. Taller species, in particular, are cut back after flowering.

☼ In summer a well-lit, slightly shaded spot; in winter in the best possible light

🌡 Moderate (10–16°C (50–61°F) at night); during the dormant season a minimum temperature of 10°C (50°F)

💧 Water moderately; sparingly in winter

💨 Moderate humidity

🪴 Somewhat chalky soil; good drainage is important

Kalanchoe (continued)

Kalanchoe tomentosa (upper photograph, foreground, right) is cared for in the same manner as *Kalanchoe blossfeldiana*. The branching stems are erect growing; the oblong leaves are densely covered in grey hairs; a few brown hairs at the top create a very unusual effect. In indoor cultivation this plant rarely, if ever, flowers. *Kalanchoe miniata* grows to 25cm (10in) and has bell-shaped flowers.

The growing instructions at the foot of p. 111 apply to all the above species; for the following species see the instructions below.

The genus *Kalanchoe* now also embraces *Bryophyllum* species. These too originate in Madagascar. *Kalanchoe laxiflora* (upper photograph, background, left) is completely covered in blue-grey bloom. The flowers are red and grow in umbels. Little plantlets may appear along the margins of the leaves.

In the lower photograph the plantlets of *Kalanchoe daigremontiana* (right) and *Kalanchoe tubiflora* (left) are clearly visible. In the latter species they appear at the extremities of the cylindrical, grey-green mottled leaves, which are slightly furrowed on the upper surface. The orange-red, bell-shaped flowers grow in cymes. The plantlets develop leaves and roots while still attached to the mother plant; they then drop.

The plants are very undemanding and easy to grow. The dry atmosphere in centrally heated homes is tolerated. In winter they need hardly be watered at all; during the growing and flowering season water normally and feed once every 3 weeks. The plants are, of course, increased from the little plantlets; in spring also from runners.

Kalanchoe uniflora is a creeping species with 2cm (¾in) long flowers, while *Kalanchoe schizophylla*, which has elongated, deeply incised leaves, is a climber suitable for a moderate greenhouse.

☼ Good light and ventilation; not in the bright midday sun

🌡 Warm (16–20°C (61–68°F) at night); keep at 10–12°C (50–54°F) in winter

💧 Avoid overwatering: this might cause rotting

🌿 Fairly tolerant of dry living-room atmosphere

🪴 Slightly chalky potting compost

Lachenalia

Cape cowslip

Lachenalia aloides bulbs flower between January and March. The most graceful form is 'Aurea'. The flower-stalks are reddish-brown and usually bear 12–18 pendulous, orange-yellow flowers, tubular in shape; the tips of the petals are sometimes slightly greenish. From May, when the foliage fades, to September the bulbs are dormant and must not be watered. In October they are potted in sandy leafmould and placed in good light in a cool position; they should still be watered only very sparingly.

Propagation can be carried out from offsets or from seed.

☼ Fairly sunny spot; enjoys fresh air

🌡 Cold (3–10°C (37–50°F) at night)

💧 Be sure to water regularly once the bulbs put forth shoots; provide good drainage

💨 Moderate humidity

🪴 Slightly chalky, friable mixture

Lampranthus

This very popular shrub-like succulent bears a profusion of radiating flowers from June to October, especially when planted in a poor mixture, for instance 1 part loam, 3 parts sand and 1 part peat. Normally the flowers only open when the sun is shining and close in inadequate light. Propagate in the autumn from tip cuttings. They root and grow rapidly. Allow the cuttings to dry before setting them in the growing medium. Seed may be sown in spring at 21°C (70°F); prick out when the seedlings are 2.5cm (1in) rall. The colour of Lampranthus species originating in South Africa varies from white via pink or orange to red. The photograph shows *Lampranthus blandus*.

☼ Throughout the year in the sunniest spot available; may be placed out of doors in summer

🌡 Warm (16–20°C (61–68°F) at night); slightly lower temperature acceptable—e.g., to 12°C (54°F). In winter 6°C (43°F)

💧 Water very moderately, especially at lower temperatures

💨 Very tolerant of dry living-room air

🪴 Potting compost mixed with sand

Lantana

Only *Lantana camara* hybrids (see photograph) and *Lantana montevidensis* are cultivated. The latter has recumbent stems, the former is erect growing. In their original form the flower heads are orange, but hybrids occur in yellow, pink and red. Most of the colours fade in the course of flowering. Plenty of light and adequate nourishment are the main requirements for successful cultivation. Propagation is from seed from January onwards, or from cuttings. Plants from which cuttings are to be taken should be kept at a slightly higher temperature from February onwards; the cuttings are taken at any time after April, but August is the best time. Young shoots should be nipped out.

☼ A sunny spot; ventilate from time to time. In summer place out of doors

🌡 Cold to moderate (5–15°C (41–59°F) at night); resting period (in a cool, airy place) at 8°C (46°F); from March onwards increase to about 12°C (54°F)

💧 Water moderately but regularly

🌫 Moderate humidity

🏺 Slightly chalky mixture

Laurus

Bay tree

The photograph shows *Laurus nobilis* planted in tubs in front of a house on an Amsterdam canal. This tree-like, dioecious shrub originates in the Mediterranean area. It is not winter-hardy, although it likes a very cold position in winter. Too high a temperature in spring will cause it to shoot too rapidly and make it susceptible to disease and pests. Start feeding before the new growth appears in spring and continue until September.

Cuttings may be taken in spring as well as in the autumn; they are rooted in equal parts of sand and peat at a bottom temperature of 16–20°C (61–68°F).

☼ A sunny position; in summer it may (depending upon the weather) be placed outside from May to October

🌡 Moderate (10–16°C (50–61°F) at night); temperature in winter 1–6°C (34–43°F)

💧 Fairly freely in the growing season; in winter beware of overwatering which will cause the leaves to turn yellow

🌫 Spray regularly

🏺 Normal proprietary potting compost

Lilium

Lily

The photograph shows a number of well known *Lilium* species and hybrids.

If you wish them to flower in spring, the bulbs must be potted in the autumn. Make sure that the pot or tub is sufficiently wide and deep and provide good drainage in the form of a layer of pebbles at the bottom. This is followed by soil mixture and a thin layer of sand on which the bulb is placed; the pot is then filled up to just above the tip of the bulb. Keep frost-free in winter and from early March onwards increase the temperature a little. Once the bulb starts into growth the temperature should be gradually increased to 18°C (64°F).

☼ Half-shade or sun

🌡 Cold (3–10°C (37–50°F) at night); lilies dislike warm feet and should never be placed over a source of heat

💧 Water moderately; normally in the growing and flowering seasons

💨 Moderate humidity

🪣 A mixture of equal parts of leafmould, sand and peat, plus one tablespoonful of bonemeal per pot

Liriope

In Europe this lily-like plant is as yet little known, but you might be able to get hold of one. The best known species is *Liriope muscari* which has bright violet flower spikes and strap-shaped leaves (see photograph). There is also a slightly smaller species, *Liriope spicata,* which puts forth runners and has small, pale pink flowers. These natives of eastern Asia flower late in summer. The berries which follow keep well.

In summer *Liriope* plants may be placed out of doors; they should be watered moderately and fed every fortnight.

Propagation by division of the root system; the sections are potted in friable soil.

☼ Tolerates some shade, but prefers good light, especially in summer

🌡 Moderate (10–16°C (50–61°F) at night); 10–12°C (50–54°F) in the dormant season

💧 Keep moderately moist; do not let the soil-ball dry out

💨 Moderate humidity

🪣 Normal pre-packed potting compost

Lithops

Living stone

As you will see in the photograph, *Lithops* is a quite remarkable looking plant. This succulent consists of two very thick leaves, joined at the base. During the dormant season, from November to April, a new pair of leaves grows from the old, which will eventually shrivel up. In September and October radiating flowers appear in the groove at the top; as a rule these are yellow or white.

Propagation is from seed; the plants will flower in 2–3 years. Pot in a porous mixture consisting of clay, leafmould and fine gravel.

☼　Keep in the best available light throughout the year

🌡　Moderate (10–16°C (50–61°F) at night); in winter allow the plant to rest at 5–8°C (41–46°F)

💧　In the growing season water extremely sparingly; keep dry in winter

💨　Low humidity is excellent

🪣　Friable, somewhat loamy mixture, or cactus soil

Lobivia

In addition to the densely haired, yellow-flowered *Lobivia densispina* illustrated, this genus, which originates in South America, comprises more than seventy other cacti. Their appearance varies considerably: they are globular to cylindrical in shape, the spines may grow close together or dispersed and may be long or short, etc. As a rule they flower freely, producing large numbers of blooms varying in colour from white via yellow to red. Some well-known species are: *L. aurea*, with yellow flowers, *L. backebergii*, red, *L. haageana*, pale yellow to red, *L. jajoiana*, red with a black centre. Propagation is from seed or from cuttings.

☼　Full sun, for instance on a south-facing windowsill

🌡　Warm (16–20°C (61–68°F) at night); cool in winter (7°C (45°F))

💧　Keep moderately moist; dry in winter

💨　Low humidity

🪣　Cactus mixture with a little extra humus

Lycaste

This genus comprises approximately forty-five species of tropical epiphyte orchids, originating in Central America. Some of these species, including the *Lycaste virginalis* illustrated, may be grown indoors with little difficulty. The fragrant *Lycaste aromatica* is a native of Mexico; it has yellow-orange flowers, small but profuse. *Lycaste cruenta* produces orange or greenish-yellow flowers, large, but few in number. When the pseudo-bulbs are fully developed they should be given a rest. Between March and May they are potted and kept in a fairly cool and shady spot until September. Reduce watering when the leaves have dropped.

☼ Half-shady position in summer; provide more light in winter

🌡 Moderate (10–16°C (50–61°F) at night); cooler in winter: around 7°C (45°F)

💧 Water regularly in the growing period; never allow the pseudo-bulbs to shrivel up

💨 High degree of humidity, but never spray

🪴 Orchid mixture

Mammillaria

Nipple cactus

This cactus genus comprises more than two hundred species, most of them natives of sunny Mexico. This means that most *Mammillaria* cacti require as much light and sunshine as possible throughout the year. Nevertheless there are a few pale green species—containing a large amount of chlorophyll—which in summer need to be screened from bright sunlight to some extent.

The plants are best watered from the bottom; in white-haired species it is particularly important to avoid the plant itself getting wet. Feed regularly in summer.

☼ Plenty of sun in summer; turn round occasionally to prevent the plant growing to one side

🌡 Warm (16–20°C (61–68°F) at night); cool in winter (7°C (45°F))

💧 Water regularly in summer, preferably in the morning; make sure that the plant does not dry out in winter

💨 Stands up well to dry living-room atmosphere

🪴 Rich, chalky cactus mixture

117

Mammillaria (continued)

Propagation is from seed in April or May, at a temperature of 21°C (70°F). Some species produce offsets; these can of course be rooted separately. Do not forget to allow them to dry for 2 or 3 days before potting them. *Mammillaria* cacti should be re-potted every year in April, in a nutritious mixture containing, among other elements, loam, sand and some leafmould and peat. Nipple cacti are very popular because they flower so readily and are so undemanding. In many cases the spines, too, are very attractive. *Mammillaria centricirrha* (see photograph on p. 117, centre) is a blue-green, more or less spherical cactus containing a milky liquid. In this species, as well as in *Mammillaria magnimamma* (upper photograph, right), the nipples are very conspicuous. In both species the flowers grow in a circle round the crown. *Mammillaria dawsonii* (photograph p. 117, left) has beautiful spines and carmine flowers. *Mammillaria herrerae* (photograph p. 117, right) is a small species with proportionally large flowers.

In the spherical *Mammillaria hahniana* (upper photograph, left) the spines are conspicuously long. Older specimens frequently grow into a more elongated shape. The flowers are deep red. *Mammillaria gracilis* var. *fragilis* (lower photograph, left) remains a fragile, tiny cactus throughout its life. It is densely covered in relatively long thorns. The flowers, creamy to yellow, are fairly inconspicuous. *Mammillaria spinossissima* (lower photograph, right) is very densely thorned and gives a prickly and woolly impression. For this species chalky soil is essential; like *Mammillaria rhodantha* it must be kept out of full sun. *Mammillaria prolifera* or sprouting *Mammillaria* forms clumps and has yellow flowers.

☼ Plenty of sun in summer; turn occasionally to prevent a lopsided shape; good light in winter

🌡 Warm (16–20°C (61–68°F) at night); keep at 6–8°C (43–46°F) in winter

💧 Water regularly in winter, preferably in the morning; in winter take care that the plant does not dry out

🌬 Stands up well to dry living-room atmosphere

🏺 Rich, chalky cactus mixture

Maranta

Arrowroot plant

This genus grows wild in the rain forests of Brazil, chiefly in open spaces. It is one of our finest foliage plants, frequently used in combination with other plants. The Maranta is sometimes nicknamed 'Prayer plant', because the leaves fold at night.

Maranta leuconeura 'Kerchoveana' (lower photograph) has purplish-brown blotches—usually ten in number—on the bright green leaves. The 'Fascinator' strain (upper photograph) is another plant that is easily obtainable. The foliage is red-veined on a velvety green, mottled background.

The leaves of *Maranta bicolor* have 6–8 brown blotches on a dark green background and are purple on the reverse.

In all species the flowers are rather inconspicuous. As *Maranta* plants produce runners, they make useful groundcover.

The plants must be re-potted every year in April, preferably in a mixture of woodland soil or leafmould, peat fibre and well-rotted cow manure, which, with the addition of a little sharp sand, produces a porous potting compost rich in humus. It is advisable to use wide, shallow bowls, so that the foliage hangs over the moist soil. From May to September feed every fortnight and spray frequently. Spraying is also beneficial in winter; in that case less water need be given.

Always use tepid water with a pH of 4–4.5. No excess water must be allowed to collect in the pot, but at the same time be careful not to let the soil-ball dry out. From September to February allow the plant to rest. Propagation is by division in spring. From May to August cuttings may be taken. Three shoots, each with two or three leaves, are potted together in a mixture of equal parts of sand and peat, at a temperature of 21°C (70°F). When rooted they are re-potted separately.

☼ A plant for a half-shady position; good light acceptable

🌡 Warm (16–20°C (61–68°F) at night); daytime temperature in winter 18–20°C (64–68°F), with a minimum of 14°C (57°F) at night

💧 In the growing season water freely, using tepid, soft water. Water less at lower temperatures

💦 Fairly high degree of humidity desirable; spray regularly

🥤 Proprietary potting compost

Medinilla

Medinilla magnifica has large, leathery dark green leaves, depressed veins and very striking flowers. The pendulous plumes consist of large pink bracts surrounding numerous little pink flowers. The total inflorescence may grow to 40cm (16in). As a rule flowering occurs between February and August. In the growing season the plant should be fed every fortnight. After the dormant season from November till the end of January it may be cut back a little and re-potted. Do not feed until the flower-buds are visible. Propagation is by air-layering or from cuttings rooted in sand and peat, with a bottom heat of 25–30°C (77–86°F).

☼ Well-lit position, out of full sun

🌡 Warm (16–20°C (61–68°F) at night); keep at 15–17°C (59–63°F) in the dormant season

💧 Water fairly freely in the growing period, using soft, tepid water; less thereafter

💦 Spray (including the reverse of the leaves) to provide a high degree of humidity; or use the deep-plate method

🪴 Nutritious and friable soil, e.g. bromeliad mixture

Microcoelum

Coconut palm

Microcoelum weddelianum (illustrated) has gracefully curving, feathery leaves, which may grow to 1.50m (5ft) in length. The narrow side-leaves are grey on the reverse. The stem is surrounded by brown fibres. Drying of the soil-ball and inadequate humidity are the main causes of dying leaf tips. If the plant turns yellow it means that it is standing in too cold a position. This palm must be kept indoors throughout the year, a little cooler in winter. In the growing season feed every ten days or so. The palms prefer a tall pot, not too large.
  Propagation is from seed.

☼ Well-lit position, out of full sun

🌡 Warm in summer (16–20°C (61–68°F) at night); keep at 15–18°C (59–64°F) in winter

💧 The soil-ball must never dry out; in the growing season water frequently, using soft water

💦 High degree of humidity in summer

🪴 Standard proprietary potting compost (slightly acid)

Microlepia

This fern has a feathery, soft bright green foliage and is a native of the tropics. The only species grown as a house plant is *Microlepia speluncae* and its special strain 'Cristata', of which the leaves broaden at the tip.

If necessary, re-pot in spring in a tall pot. *Microlepia* requires a richer mixture than other ferns. In the growing season water freely and give a small feed every fortnight. In winter maintain a minimum temperature of 15°C (59°F), water less and do not feed. Propagation is from spores.

 Slight or deep shade, according to choice

 Moderate (10–16°C (50–61°F) at night)

 Water freely, using soft water; plunging several times a week is excellent

 Ferns enjoy a humid atmosphere; spray often

 A mixture rich in humus, e.g. 3 parts leafmould, 2 parts rotted cow manure and 1 part coarse sand

Mimosa

Sensitive plant

The photograph shows what happens when, in the daytime, at a minimum temperature of 18°C (64°F), a *Mimosa pudica* is touched: the feathery pinnate leaves fold immediately. At night they are folded as well.

The plants are easily grown from seed in March; germination takes 12–15 days. The most vigorous of the seedlings are cultivated; do not pinch out the tip. In the growing season and during the flowering period which follows soon after, water freely and feed every fortnight. As a rule the plant flowers between June and October.

Mimosa dislikes smoke.

 Requires fairly good light and ventilation; keep out of the sun

 Warm (16–20°C (61–68°F) at night)

 Water regularly and prevent the soil-ball drying out

 Requires a fairly high degree of humidity; spray regularly

Slightly chalky potting compost

121

Monstera

Swiss cheese plant

This genus embraces about fifty species, which grow wild in Central and South America. They are evergreen climbers which, in addition to their normal roots, develop aerial roots that change into ordinary roots as soon as they touch the soil. In youth the leaves are smooth-edged, the incisions appearing at a later stage, followed by the perforations; these latter appear only if the plant is given adequate light and nourishment. The photograph shows the *Monstera deliciosa*, which originates on the western slopes of the Mexican mountains. The leaves are thick, leathery and slashed with one or more deep incisions. Mature plants produce an unusual inflorescence, consisting of a creamy bract and a spadix on which berries are developed; these smell of pineapple.

The 'Borgsiana' variety is slightly smaller than the species in all its parts. Among other strains in cultivation are: *Monstera obliqua*, which has oblong perforations and unincised leaf-edges; *Monstera accuminata*, in which mature leaves are large, asymmetrical and deeply slashed; and *Monstera pertusa*, a rapid climber with dense foliage.

Propagation is by air-layering or from cuttings or seed. As a rule tip shoots are used for cuttings, but it is also possible to take stem sections, preferably with an eye and one or more aerial roots. In the case of tip cuttings the growing point is used, together with a mature leaf. They are rooted in bottom heat.

Monstera is an undemanding plant and stands up well to temperature variations. It will be at its most attractive if placed in a well-lit and humid environment.

Mature plants should be re-potted every two or three years in a friable, porous and nutritious mixture, rich in humus. Yellowing of the leaf tips may indicate either too much or too little water.

- ☼ Satisfied with little light
- Warm (16–20°C (61–68°F) at night); keep a little cooler in winter (minimum 10°C (50°F))
- ⬥ Water moderately but regularly, so that the soil does not dry out entirely
- Moderate humidity; occasionally spray and sponge the foliage
- Normal to chalky mixture

Myrtus

Myrtle

Myrtus communis (see photograph) is the best known representative of this genus, which originates in the Mediterranean area. The evergreen shrub has shiny, leathery leaves and little round flowers, conspicuous by their large numbers of protruding stamens. Both the flowers and the foliage are fragrant. Flowering occurs between June and September; in the autumn the flowers are succeeded by berries, blue-black or white, depending on the strain. Propagation from seed or from unripe, 10cm (4in) tip cuttings; these are dipped in rooting powder and rooted in a cold frame.

 Place out of doors in summer; a well-lit, roomy position out of the sun throughout the rest of the year

 Cold to moderate (5–14°C (41–57°F) at night); in winter: 2–5°C (36–41°F) at night, up to 10°C (50°F) during the day

 Water sufficiently to prevent the soil-ball drying out, but avoid excess water in the pot

 Moderate humidity

Nutritious potting compost rich in humus

Narcissus

In addition to the *Narcissus* 'Cragford' with its white flowers and orange crowns (see photograph), the well-known 'Paperwhite' with all-white flowers is also very suitable for indoor cultivation. 'Paperwhites' may be set in shallow bowls filled with pebbles from September till January. The water must not touch the bulbs, for this would cause decay. 'Paperwhites' may be placed in the light from the beginning, but other species must root in the dark at a temperature of 8–10°C (46–50°F) in a mixture of equal parts of sand and potting compost; they are brought into the light only when the bud has left the bulb.

 Well-lit, airy situation

 Cold (3–10°C (37–50°F) at night; the flowers will last much longer in a very moderately heated room

 Water moderately but regularly

 Moderate humidity; where the atmosphere is dry mist-spray frequently

 Proprietary potting compost or pebbles

Neoporteria

This is a genus of spherical cacti which may become somewhat cylindrical at a more advanced age, but will always remain fairly small. They originate in Chile and northern Argentina. The thorns are usually very beautiful; they vary in colour from white via yellow and brown to black. *Neoporteria subgibbosa* (illustrated) has up to twenty ribs subdivided by notches. The flowers are pink and yellow. Other species are *Neoporteria nidus*, *N. napina* and *N. senilis*—the latter resembles the old man cactus. *Neoporteria* cacti grow slowly and are therefore often grafted.

☼ Good light in winter and as much sun as possible in summer

🌡 Warm (16–20°C (61–68°F) at night); keep cool in winter at 6–8°C (43–46°F)

○ Water normally in summer, then gradually decrease; keep completely dry in winter

💦 Spray thoroughly in high temperatures

🪴 Special cactus mixture

Neoregelia

This bromeliad is from Brazil, and develops tubular rosettes and long, fairly narrow leaves, often beautifully coloured. The foliage surrounding the short flower-stalks, which do not emerge from the tube, is often very brightly coloured, as may be seen in the photograph. The best known species is *Neoregelia carolinae* (illustrated), whose outer leaves are green, the inner red. In the 'Tricolor' strain the green leaves have a longitudinal yellow stripe. *Neoregelia concentrica* forms large rosettes of prickly, dark-mottled leaves and has violet-coloured bracts.

☼ Good light, but keep out of direct sunlight

🌡 Warm (16–20°C (61–68°F) at night); 15–18°C (59–64°F) in winter

○ Water normally; in very high temperatures water freely

💦 High degree of humidity desirable

🪴 Special bromeliad soil; this may, for instance, be composed of sphagnum and rotted leaves

Nephrolepis

Ladder fern; sword fern

This genus, found everywhere in the tropics and sub-tropics, comprises about thirty species of ferns. *Nephrolepis cordifolia* is terrestrial growing as well as epiphytic; its creeping rootstock develops runners with 2–5cm ($\frac{3}{4}$–2in) thick tubers; these serve as reserve organs. The fronds grow up to 60cm (24in) and are doubly pinnate. In the 'Plumosa' strain the individual leaf sections are pinnate in turn. The best known ladder fern for indoor cultivation is *Nephrolepis exaltata*, of which numerous ornamental strains exist. The species develops neither runners nor tubers; the fronds may grow to 1m (40in) in length. In the photograph you see at the back the strain 'Rooseveltii Plumosa', with doubly pinnate fronds and pinnate or crisped leaves. Single-feathered strains are 'Rooseveltii' (centre) and 'Teddy Junior' (below). The many ornamental forms are fairly similar.

Propagation is from spores, by planting runners, or by division. This is best done in spring, though runners may be detached from the mother plant in summer as well. Grow in a mixture of equal parts of sand and fibrous peat, and subsequently transfer to a mixture of 3 parts peat or leafmould, 2 parts loam and 1 part sand, to which a little sphagnum and cow manure may be added.

Living-room air is often too dry for *Nephrolepis*. The deep-saucer method or an evaporator may solve the problem. It is also important to feed regularly and generously—once a week—and to water adequately in the growing period. If the plant deteriorates in spite of your attentions it should be given a rest with less water and no fertiliser; remove ugly foliage. After about five weeks give a little more water, re-pot if necessary, and try to bring the fern into growth again. Decrease the water supply in winter and give a small feed once a month.

☼ Will take a fair amount of light (no direct sunlight), but also tolerates shade

🌡 Moderate (10–16°C (50–61°F) at night); minimum temperature in winter 14°C (57°F)

💧 Keep the soil moist throughout the year; water fairly often in the growing season

💨 Ensure a high degree of humidity

🏺 Nutritious, friable soil, rich in humus

Nerium

Oleander

Nerium oleander (illustrated) is a poisonous evergreen shrub with lancet-shaped leaves growing in groups of three. The flowers appear in terminal clusters; in this case they are single and pink, but there are also double forms and the colour may be white, red or even yellow.

In Mediterranean countries, the oleander's native habitat, the plant can spend the winter outside, but elsewhere it must be brought indoors. Propagation is from tip shoots; these will root even in water. Take care when potting them. Feed weekly in the growing season.

 Always the sunniest spot available; in summer it may be placed in a sheltered position out of doors

 Warm (16–20°C (61–68°F) at night); will stand up to a few degrees of frost; temperature in winter 4–6°C (39–43°F)

 Water generously in summer, using tepid water; does not mind a footbath

 Tolerant of dry air

Somewhat loamy potting compost

Nertera

Bead plant

This little plant, a native of South America, is grown for its orange berries which follow the inconspicuous flowers—April to June—in such large numbers that the leaves are practically invisible. They may last for several months.

Increase from seed in February-March in sandy soil; or by division in August. Pot in a well-drained mixture. Feed sparingly, using a nitrogen-free fertiliser to avoid excessive leaf development.

The correct specific name is *Nertera granadensis*.

 Requires a fair amount of light, but does not tolerate full sun; place in an airy spot

 Moderate (10–16°C (50–61°F) at night)

 Water moderately from the bottom

 Requires a high degree of humidity; provide this not by spraying but by the deep-saucer method
Sandy mixture rich in humus; pot in half-size pots, for the plant has a shallow root system

Nidularium

This genus originates in Brazil and comprises more than twenty species, of which about ten are in cultivation. All species develop rosettes. As a rule the central leaves of these epiphytes are vividly coloured. The curving leaves of *Nidularium fulgens* widen at the base and are up to 30cm (12in) in length, prickly, and with green blotches. Little violet-coloured flowers grow in the axils of the red bracts. *Nidularium innocentii* (illustrated) has dark olive-green leaves, purplish-brown on the reverse. Before the plant comes into flower the central leaves are bright red; the flowers are creamy. Propagation from seed or from runners.

 Slight or semi-shade

 Warm (16–20°C (61–68°F) at night); maintain a constant temperature, especially in the growing season

 Water generously in summer; water may be poured over the plant

 High degree of humidity

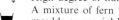 A mixture of fern roots, sphagnum moss and leaf-mould; or special bromeliad mixture

Notocactus

This genus embraces 15 species, natives of South America. Usually these cacti are spherical in shape, with ribs divided into knobs. Both the spines and the yellow (sometimes red) flowers growing from the crown are very fine. These cacti are extremely easy to grow and even young plants soon flower profusely. The species photographed is *Notocactus ottonis*, which has a bright green globular body which may develop offsets. The thorns are yellow- to red-brown. The yellow flowers, 4cm (1½in) in diameter, appear from May to July. Other species: *Notocactus apricus*, *Notocactus concinnus* and *Notocactus scopa*.

 Out of doors or in a fairly sunny position indoors in summer

 Warm (16–20°C (61–68°F) at night); minimum temperature in winter 10°C (50°F)

 Keep moist in summer, using soft water; avoid stagnant water in the pot

 Spray in the growing period; otherwise keep dry

 Nutritious, friable and acid soil

Odontoglossum

The more than two hundred epiphytic, tropical orchids included in this genus originate in Central and South America, where they grow in a damp, cool environment on the edges of mountain forests, usually· at altitudes of between 1,500 and 3,000m (5,000–10,000ft). The pseudo-tubers vary in shape; they are single- or double-lobed and at the base surrounded by leaves, from which the flowerstalk, often fairly tall, develops.

Odontoglossum bictoniense (upper photograph) in winter puts forth a flowerstalk up to 1m (40in) in length, bearing 3–4 flowers. The petals are yellowish-green with dark blotches; the lip is pink. *Odontoglossum grande* (lower photograph), a native of Guatemala, has broad, oval pseudo-tubers and a flowerstalk of up to 40cm (16in), which from October to December bears 4–8 yellow and brown flowers more than 15cm (6in) across. Other species suitable for living-room cultivation are: *Odontoglossum insleayi*, yellow and red, flowers in winter; *Odontoglossum pulchellum*, a small plant with fragrant yellow and red flowers; and *Odontoglossum schlieperianum*, which produces its yellow and brown flowers from July to September. All these species like a cool situation and are reasonably tolerant of a dry atmosphere. *Odontoglossum grande* is the strongest orchid for indoor cultivation. When re-potting in spring it is important to put a good layer of crocks in the bottom of the pot to ensure adequate drainage. A suitable mixture is 2 parts fern roots, 1 part decayed beech leaves and 1 part sphagnum.

Other species belonging to this genus are more suited for cultivation in a moderately cool greenhouse: they include *Odontoglossum cervantesii*, a fragrant winter-flowering form with brownish-red with white flowers, *Odontoglossum cordatum* and *Odontoglossum maculatum*.

Protect from bright sunlight; may be put out of doors in summer; or indoors in an airy spot

Moderate (10–16°C (50–61°F) at night); minimum temperature in winter 7°C (45°F)

Keep moist in the growing season, using soft water; keep dry in the dormant season

High degree of humidity in summer

Special orchid mixture

Ophiopogon

When not in flower, *Ophiopogon jaburan* bears great resemblance to *Liriope muscari* (p. 115), but *Ophiopogon* produces white flowers and red berries. The divergence from *Ophiopogon japonicus* is much more obvious; the latter has runners, curved leaves and flowerspikes lower than the foliage. The form in the photograph is *Ophiopogon jaburan* 'Vittatus', with creamy, longitudinal stripes on the leaves.

These plants are undemanding and are easily kept in good condition. Propagation is by division in spring; the sections are potted in peat-based compost.

☼ Tolerates shade

🌡 Moderate (10–16°C (50–61°F) at night); keep at 5–10°C (41–50°F) in winter
Stands up well to considerable temperature variations

💧 Water generously in the growing period, moderately in winter

🌫 Moderate humidity

🪴 Somewhat chalky soil, rich in humus

Oplismenus

This plant belongs to the family of grasses. It has bare creeping or hanging stems and pointed, wavy-edged leaves. When the stems touch the soil they will readily root, and rooted cuttings are thus easily obtainable. These are potted in a mixture of standard potting soil and some peat fibre and leafmould. Place a few cuttings together in one pot to achieve a bushy plant. In addition to the *Oplismenus hirtellus* illustrated there is a form called 'Variegatus', which has longitudinally white-striped foliage, sometimes touched with pink. Feed sparingly.

☼ A very well-lit situation in winter; slight shade in summer

🌡 Warm (16–20°C (61–68°F) at night); keep at 10–20°C (50–68°F) in winter. This means it may stay in the living-room

💧 Water generously in the growing period; decrease watering from late August onwards

🌫 Moderate humidity

🪴 Nutritious, calcareous soil, rich in humus

Opuntia

Fig cactus

This genus embraces 250 species, originally found only in the Americas, where the fruit formed an important source of nourishment for the indigenous population. Centuries ago the plants were brought to other parts of the world, where they now grow wild, so that their area of distribution is enormous. There are hardy species, such as *Opuntia compressa*, which has creeping branches and flat oval joints from which pale yellow flowers appear. *Opuntia rhodantha*, with brownish-red joints and magnificent red flowers is another hardy species, as is *Opuntia fragilis*. Flat-jointed *Opuntia* species are particularly undemanding. There are also cylindrical species as well as *Tephrocactus* species, whose joints are spherical or club-shaped. The two latter require a slightly heavier soil mixture, for instance one containing more clay. *Tephrocactus* species are sensitive to damp; they grow very slowly and for that reason are sometimes grafted onto *Austrocylinder Opuntia* forms.

Be careful when handling *Opuntia* cacti, for they may give you painful pricks.

The *Opuntia* is increased from seed or from cuttings. The joints must first be left to dry out for 2–3 days before being potted. Cuttings are taken in June or July; sowing takes place in early spring at 21°C (70°F), after the seeds have first been soaked.

In the photograph you see *Opuntia bergeriana* (foreground, right), which bears orange-red flowers and may grow very tall. *Opuntia delactiana* (background, right) has little spine development and bears orange flowers. *Opuntia microdasys* (foreground, left) is relatively slow-growing; each areole bears a tuft of golden-yellow glochids. *Opuntia scheerii* (background, left), finally, is densely spined and may grow very tall.

In summer a sunny outdoor position; keep cool and in good light in winter

Warm (16–20°C (61–68°F) at night); temperature in winter 6–8°C (43–46°F)

Moderately in the growing season; from mid-August onwards decrease the water supply; keep dry in the dormant season

Maintain low humidity

Nutritious and porous cactus mixture

Oxalis

Wood sorrel

Two of the more than eight hundred *Oxalis* species are illustrated: *Oxalis lasiandra* (left), a native of Mexico, has 5- to 9-lobed leaves, red-mottled on the reverse; these appear from small, yellowish-brown tubers. The little lilac-pink flowers grow in umbels. *Oxalis deppei* (right), the lucky four-leaved clover, has rose-red flowers in summer and autumn. The bright green leaves are crossed by a pink stripe. At night the leaves fold along the centre vein.

Tubers may be potted from January onwards; or they may be planted out of doors from April onwards.

☼   Well-lit, sunny situation

🌡   Cool to moderate (6–12°C (43–54°F) at night); the daytime temperature should preferably not exceed 18°C (64°F)

💧   Water very moderately; it is easy to give too much, which will cause the stems to grow lanky

☁   Moderate humidity

🪣   Friable, loamy soil. Until August feed once a week

Pachyphytum

This is a genus of succulents originating in Mexico. *Pachyphytum oviferum* (photograph, left) has short stems with a rosette of thick, oval leaves, covered in white bloom. The bell-shaped flowers are deep red. *Pachyphytum hookerii* (right) is very squat in habit and has blue-green bloomed leaves and red and yellow bell-shaped flowers. Crossing *Pachyphytum* and *Echeveria* resulted in × *Pachyveria* (centre), which is described on p. 133. Propagation is from seed, or from leaf- or tip cuttings (especially if a plant has grown bare); these have to dry out first.

☼   Airy, sunny spot in summer; in winter it should have plenty of light as well

🌡   Moderate (10–16°C (50–61°F) at night); keep at 6–10°C (43–50°F) in winter, in proportion to the available light

💧   Keep fairly dry throughout the year

☁   Stands up very well to dry living-room air; avoid water on bloomed foliage

🪣   Sandy and humusy mixture

Pachypodium

The twenty species belonging to this genus are natives of South Africa, Angola and Madagascar, where they live in deserts and steppes. Accordingly they have thick, often tuberous, fleshy stems. True trunk-forming species are often thorny; the leaves grow in rosettes at the top, as shown in the photograph of *Pachypodium lameri*. The flowers, as a rule very striking, occur in shades of yellow, pink or red. The sap of these plants is extremely poisonous.

Propagation is from seed, which germinates in sandy soil at a high temperature.

☼ A well-lit, sunny spot throughout the year

🌡 Warm (16–20°C (61–68°F) at night); in winter the temperature should be 14–16°C (57–61°F)

💧 Water moderately in the main growing season, winter; keep fairly dry in summer

🌫 Low to moderate humidity

🪣 Friable, loamy mixture in well-draining, deep pots

Pachystachys

The *Pachystachys lutea* illustrated is today widely marketed once more. It originates in the region between Mexico and Brazil. The plant resembles the *Aphelandra*, but has softer, plain green leaves. The inflorescence, 15cm (6in) long, is covered in a number of lemon-yellow bracts which stay for several weeks. The white flowers soon drop. In spring the plant should be cut back a little. It is easily increased from cuttings. Shoots or stem cuttings may be rooted from mid-January until the end of July; the young plants should have the tips pinched out more than once to produce a bushy shape.

☼ Good light, possibly diffused sunlight, but avoid bright sun

🌡 Warm (16–20°C (61–68°F) at night); 10–15°C (50–59°F) in winter

💧 Water generously in the growing period and plunge from time to time; be very sparing with water in the dormant season

🌫 Likes a fairly high degree of humidity; less so at lower temperatures

🪣 A loamy, humusy mixture; pre-packed potting compost

× Pachyveria

This hybrid genus is the result of crossing *Echeveria* and *Pachyphytum*. The photograph shows × *Pachyveria scheideckeri*, with spatulate blue-green and white-bloomed foliage and an inflorescence consisting of bracts, which drop, and orange flowers. In summer these succulents may be put out of doors in a sunny position. In winter they must be kept cool and dry.

Propagation is from tip-cuttings, leaf-cuttings or side-shoots, which must be left to dry before being set in a mixture of peat fibre and sand, or in pure sand.

☼	May be placed in a sunny outdoor position in summer; plenty of light in winter
🌡	Moderate (10–16°C (50–61°F) at night); keep cool in winter
💧	Water moderately in summer; keep practically dry in the dormant season
	Dry to moderately humid air
	Mixture of leafmould, clay and sand

Pandanus

Screw pine

This genus comprises more than six hundred species of tropical evergreen shrubs and trees. The *Pandanus veitchii* illustrated is a native of Polynesia. The strap-shaped green leaves are prickly and have longitudinal cream-coloured stripes. This species is the one most often grown indoors, as it stands up well to dry air. Mature specimens develop offsets at the base; these may be removed to grow new plants. Treat the cut surface with charcoal powder and root the cuttings in bottom heat (25–30°C (77–86°F)).

☼	Good light, no direct sunlight
🌡	Warm (16–20°C (61–68°F) at night); minimum temperature in winter 18°C (64°F)
💧	Water generously in the growing season, using slightly demineralised, tepid water; water less in winter
	Likes a humid atmosphere
	Proprietary potting compost or, better still, a mixture of leafmould, peat and rotted turves

Paphiopedilum

Venus' slipper

The representatives of this genus, which embraces over fifty species, are immediately recognisable by the slipper-shaped lip. Most of these terrestrial-growing orchids originate in Asia. They have an underground rootstock without pseudo-bulbs; the roots are fleshy. The leaves develop from the base; they are leathery and may be plain green, mottled or marbled. As a rule the flower-stalk bears only one flower. The upper sepal is called the flag; the two side sepals remain small. The side petals are often elongated and of the same colour as the lip. The flowers last for a long time.

Green-leaved species are re-potted around February, others in June. Instead of re-potting it is sometimes sufficient to replace the upper layer of soil. When watering be careful that the roots do not rot. In September place in slightly better light. Most *Paphiopedilum* species form flower-buds in October; dry air is harmful to this process. In November maintain the temperature at about 14°C (57°F) and decrease the water supply a little. In December water twice a week, but maintain a humid atmosphere—the living-room is usually too dry. The following are some of the green-leaved species suitable for a moderately heated greenhouse: *Paphiopedilum fairieanum*, with white flowers striped with green and purple; *Paphiopedilum hirsutissimum*, very hairy with flowers of green, purple and brown, the colours merging into one another; *Paphiopedilum insigne*, a well-known orchid, whose flowers are greenish-white with reddish-brown, which must be grown in a very cool environment; *Paphiopedilum villosum*, which produces white/green/brown flowers between December and April. There are numerous hybrids. *Paphiopedilum × nitens* (see photograph) is the result of crossing *P. insigne* and *P. villosum*.

☼   Shady situation

🌡   15°C (59°F; night), 25–30°C (77–86°F; day); in winter 15–18°C (59–64°F) at night and 18–20°C (64–68°F) during the daytime. Species with multi-coloured foliage a little warmer

💧   Water normally, using soft water; no real dormant season, but give a little less water in winter

💨   Ensure a humid atmosphere

🪴   Orchid mixture

Parodia

This genus of spherical cacti comprises about forty different species, very popular because they flower profusely, have beautiful spines and present few problems in cultivation. They should, however, be watered carefully for the root-neck is very sensitive to water. Propagation is from seed; in a few cases from cuttings.

  Parodia aureispina (photograph) is a native of northern Argentina. This cactus is densely spined with barbed central thorns and smaller, straight side thorns. The flowers are golden-yellow. *Parodia chrysacanthion* has yellow spines and flowers, *Parodia nivosa* white spines and red flowers.

☼ Very sunny in summer; cool and in good light in winter; seedlings must be protected against bright sunlight

🌡 Warm (16–20°C (61–68°F) at night); keep at 8–12°C (46–54°F) in winter

💧 Water very sparingly; keep dry in winter

Low humidity

Cactus mixture or leafmould mixed with sand and crushed potsherds

Passiflora

Passion flower

The passion flower owes its name to the unusual shape of its inflorescence, which has been seen as a symbol of the Passion of Christ.

  The *Passiflora violacea* illustrated is not quite so well known as *Passiflora caerulea*, which is often grown on walls. The flowers are greenish-white, with blue-white and purple circles; the fruits are orange. Another species suitable for indoor cultivation is *Passiflora racemosa*, which has orange flower umbels and threefold leaves.

  Do not worry if the leaves turn yellow and drop provided some foliage remains.

☼ Will flower only in a warm and sunny spot

🌡 Moderate (10–16°C (50–61°F) at night); be sure to keep cool (5–10°C (41–50°F)) in winter; may be put out of doors

💧 Water normally in the growing and flowering seasons; decrease at the approach of autumn

Moderate humidity

Heavy, nutritious, chalky soil, rich in humus. Too light a mixture will prevent flowering

Pavonia

The one hundred and seventy species of this genus occur in many countries, but only the *Pavonia multiflora* illustrated, a native of Brazil, has achieved the status of a house plant. This winter-flowering plant grows in the form of a shrub, usually single-stemmed with lancet-shaped evergreen foliage. The flowers grow in the axils of the leaves in erect, terminal racemes. The leaves of the reddish-purple involucrum are linear in shape, curving at the tip. The purple corolla never opens; the stamens appear before flowering. Propagation from tip cuttings in bottom heat (30°C (80°F)) in a mixture of peat fibre and sand.

☼ Prefers a half-shady position

🌡 Warm (16–20°C (61–68°F) at night); keep at 12–18°C (54–64°F) in winter. Place in a warmer spot when the plant starts into growth

💧 Plenty of water in the flowering period; feed every fortnight. Water sparingly in the dormant season

🌦 Spray occasionally; fairly humid air

🪣 Peat-based potting compost

Pelargonium

Geranium

The majority of *Pelargonium* species in cultivation originate in South Africa. There are about two hundred and fifty species in all, some of which may be grown out of doors. *Pelargonium grandiflorum* (photograph left) is a true house plant; this is the French geranium which flowers from April to September. In the growing and flowering seasons it should be fed every week.

Ensure that no stagnant water remains in the pot, for this is something a geranium does not tolerate. Propagation is from tip cuttings in August.

☼ Very good light; screen against over-bright midday sun

🌡 Moderate (10–16°C (50–61°F) at night); keep cool in winter at 10–15°C (50–59°F), in not too dark a spot

💧 From March to August water freely, using slightly demineralised water, then gradually decrease; finally water sparingly

🌦 Likes fresh air

🪣 Chalky, compost-based soil

Pelargonium (continued)

The widest colour range is found among the *Pelargonium zonale* hybrids (photograph, left). When bruised, the leaves have a distinctive scent; another characteristic is the reddish-brown circle on the foliage. These plants flower from April to October and are very suitable for use as bedding plants. *Pelargonium peltatum* hybrids (right) have shiny, ivy-like foliage and a creeping or hanging habit. From among the group of scented geraniums we have photographed *Pelargonium radens* (photograph on p. 136, right). The pinnate leaves are lemon- or rose-scented; the flowers are white, red or pink. This is grown from cuttings taken in spring.

☼ Out of doors in summer. *P. zonale* may be placed in full sun, *P. peltatum* prefers half-shade

🌡 Moderate (10–16°C (50–61°F) at night); keep cool in winter (6–8°C (43–46°F)), for instance in a cellar

💧 Freely in the growing season; very sparingly in winter

💨 Likes fresh air

🪣 Well-draining, chalky soil

Pellaea

This genus occupies a special place among ferns, for *Pellaea* has leathery leaves and therefore stands up reasonably well to a dry living-room atmosphere. The species illustrated is *Pellaea rotundifolia* with singly pinnate leaves; this is a well-known house plant, fairly low-growing and of spreading habit. *Pellaea viridis* is marketed on a smaller scale. This species has doubly or trebly pinnate, elongated triangular leaves. Feed every fortnight and occasionally spray; the water need not be soft.

Propagation is from spores or, much easier, by division. Pot in a fern mixture or in standard proprietary potting compost.

☼ Satisfied with little light; never place in full sun

🌡 Moderate (10–16°C (50–61°F) at night). Can stay in a heated room in winter (minimum 10°C (50°F))

💧 Maintain constant moisture; be careful the soil-ball does not dry out

💨 Stands up reasonably well to dry living-room air

🪣 Well-drained potting compost, rich in humus

Pellionia

Pellionia species originally inhabited the tropical rain forests of south-eastern Asia. Two of them are at present in cultivation. The leaves of *Pellionia repens* (photograph) are pale green in the centre and dark brown along the margin; the initially erect growing stems later become pendulous. *Pellionia pulchra* has the same habit but its foliage is much darker; pale green blotches appear only along the veins. The underside of the leaves is purple.

Cuttings are rooted in bottom heat in spring. Pot in well-drained bowls. Feed weekly in the growing period. Beware of draughts.

☼ Well-lit to moderately shady position

🌡 Warm (16–20°C (61–68°F) at night); keep at a minimum of 10–12°C (50–54°F) in winter

💧 In the growing period water freely, uuing soft water; water sparingly in winter

〰 Fairly high degree of humidity

🥣 Friable, nutritious soil, rich in humus

Peperomia

Nearly all the species of this genus are tropical or sub-tropical herbaceous plants originating in Central and South America, where they grow as epiphytes on treetrunks or branches, or terrestrially in the rain forest. About one thousand species are known to date, most of them with very decorative foliage. Many species and strains are suitable for use indoors, especially in bottle gardens.

These plants are so-called leaf- and stem-succulents; in other words, like true succulents, they are able to store a reserve water supply in these organs, although in *Peperomia* the leaves are not so obviously thickened. In practice this means that we must be very careful with watering. As long as the foliage does not shrivel up the plant will not dry out.

The photograph on this page shows the well-known *Peperomia caperata* (left), which has strongly crispate dark green leaves, pale green on the reverse. The leaf- and flowerstalks are rose-red, the spikes are white. The leaves of *Peperomia verticillata* (right) grow in fours around the stem.

Peperomia (continued)

Peperomia argyreia (upper photograph, foreground) has shield-shaped fleshy leaves with silvery marking between the veins. The flower- and leafstalks are red. The leaves of *Peperomia arifolia* are similar in shape, but are monochrome dark green. *Peperomia blanda* has reddish-brown, erect growing stems and is covered in short hairs. The leaves grow in fours and are red on the reverse. *Peperomia glabella* has trailing stems and can therefore be used as a hanging plant. *Peperomia incana* has thick, fleshy leaves, white and felty on both surfaces. *Peperomia maculosa* has reddish-brown mottled leafstalks and dark green leaves with a white centre vein. The leaves of *Peperomia obtusifolia* (lower photograph, centre) are short-stalked, densely growing, thick and fleshy; the plant has firm, bare stems and terminal spikes. 'Longenii' (lower photograph, foreground) and 'Variegata' (upper photograph, back) variegated strains and require more light than their all-green counterparts. *Peperomia resediflora*, now called *Peperomia fraseri*, is a species with small racemes of fragrant white flowers. A creeping species is *Peperomia rotundifolia*, which has circular marbled leaves and slender runners. *Peperomia serpens* has limp, bare slightly winding stems bearing widely scattered pointed green leaves. The variegated form 'Variegata' is shown in the lower photograph (background).

Propagation is from leaf- or tip-cuttings or from shoots, preferably in spring; they are rooted in bottom heat in a sandy mixture. Initially they should be kept under glass or plastic, but care must be taken that the fleshy parts do not rot. As a rule the cuttings are first left to dry.

Erect growing species may have the tips nipped out to encourage bushy growth. From May to September feed every two or three weeks.

☼ Well-lit place, out of direct sunlight

🌡 Warm (16–20°C (61–68°F) at night); variegated forms are kept at 18–20°C (64–68°F) in winter, all-green plants at 15°C (59°F)

💧 Water moderately, using tepid, soft water; very sparingly in winter

Very humid in summer, less so in winter

Light, porous soil, rich in humus

Pereskia

Leaf cactus

This genus comprises twenty shrubby cacti, of which *Pereskia aculeata* is illustrated. This is a climbing shrub with elliptical pointed leaves mottled in shades of yellow. The branches are thorny, the thorns as a rule growing singly or in twos or threes; they enable the young shoots to support themselves. Pinkish-white flowers appear in October; they have a very unpleasant smell.

Propagation is in spring from seed sown in bottom heat (21°C (70°F)). In summer half-ripe shoots may be rooted in equal parts of peat and sand. When the leaves have dropped the plant is pruned and left to rest.

 Slightly shady position with a little sun in the afternoon and evening

 Warm (16–20°C (61–68°F) at night); in winter a minimum temperature of 10°C (50°F)

 Water generously in the growing season; very little after the foliage has dropped

 Moderate humidity

 Somewhat loamy mixture, or cactus soil

Persea

Avocado

This plant is rarely obtainable from a florist's, but can be easily grown from the stone of an avocado pear, planted point down. It may also be rooted in water: insert three matchsticks halfway up the stone and place it over a glass of water.

Persea americana (photograph) may be increased from cuttings taken in spring and rooted in bottom heat. Mature indoor plants have elliptical leaves; unfortunately they do not bear fruit.

 Good light; a little sun will do no harm

 Moderate to warm (12–20°C (54–68°F) at night); temperature in winter 10–12°C (50–54°F)

 Keep the soil-ball constantly moist

 Moderate humidity; occasionally spray the foliage

 Nutritious, loamy soil

Philodendron

Together with the *Monstera* and the *Scindapsus*, the Philodendron genus belongs to the family of Araceae. It comprises 275 species, cultivated chiefly for their magnificent foliage, often unusually shaped. The inflorescence, shaped like an arum lily (see upper photograph, showing *Philodendron karstenianum*) consists of a spadix and a white or coloured sheath. In a greenhouse a *Philodendron* will often flower, but in the living-room they must be regarded purely as foliage plants.

Their original habitat is in the tropical rain forests of Central and South America. Some are vigorous climbers, with or without aerial roots; others are shrubs, with or without a stem. Frequently the leaf-shape of young plants differs from that of mature specimens. *Philodendron* plants may grow to enormous height and width, especially if given plenty of room in a greenhouse. Climbing species may be increased by air-layering or from tip-cuttings rooted in bottom heat. Pinch out the tips of the cuttings before setting them under glass. A stem section with two or three nodes may also be used as a cutting. Shrubby species can be increased from seed or by division. If you intend to divide a plant, the growing point should be removed in May; when—after about a year—the side shoots are sufficiently developed, the plant is divided in such a way that part of the parent stem remains attached to each shoot. Keep at 24°C (75°F) until the sections have rooted.

Philodendron imbe has a green or purple stem with 25–35cm (10–14in) leafstalks, bearing large, arrow-shaped leaves. The variegated form 'Variegatum' is shown in the lower photograph.

Philodendron bipinnatifidum is an erect growing species with a densely-leaved stem and heart-shaped foliage. *Philodendron laciniatum* (photograph p. 142) is a climber with divided and lobed leaves. *Philodendron elegans* is undemanding; it is a climber with deeply incised foliage. *Philodendron squamiferum* has long red leafstalks covered in scaly hairs.

The following are climbing or creeping species with individed leaves: *Philolendron elongatum*, which has elongated large leaves; *Philodendron erubescens*, whose leaves are initially dark brown, later turning green and shiny, and

Philodendron (continued)

whose sheath is red, the spadix ivory-white; and *Philodendron melanochrysum*, *Philodendron panduriforme* and *Philodendron scandens* (with fairly small, heart-shaped leaves), which are among the best known.

Philodendron martianum has a short stalk and elongated leaves. Apart from *Philodendron scandens*, which is very easy to grow, all species are to some extent sensitive as regards situation and care. While one owner will rarely encounter problems, another may find that the plants do not thrive. It is a question of trial and error. Always remember to provide adequate warmth.

☼ Never put in full sun; a fair amount of shade is tolerated

🌡 Warm (16–20°C (61–68°F) at night); in winter a minimum of 14°C (57°F) for green-leaved, and of 18°C (64°F) for variegated and velvet-leaved forms

💧 In summer give plenty of tepid water

💨 Fairly high degree of humidity is desirable

🪣 Standard to calcareous potting mixture

Phlebodium

This fern was formerly marketed under the name *Polypodium*. The *Phlebodium* genus originates in South America; the *Phlebodium aureum* illustrated is the only species. The pinnate leaves have a bluish sheen and grow on leaf-stalks up to 50cm (20in) in length. The root-stock, which eventually fills the entire pot, is light brown and scaly. The plant may grow to enormous size and sometimes becomes too large for the living-room. In that case it is best transferred to a greenhouse and given plenty of room. Propagation is by division or from seed. In the growing season give a salt-free feed.

☼ Shady position

🌡 Warm (16–20°C (61–68°F) at night); temperature in winter 18–22°C (64–70°F)

💧 Keep the soil moist, using soft water, but not too wet

💨 High degree of humidity essential, for instance by using the deep-plate method

🪣 Standard potting compost is better than a fern mixture

Phoenix

Date palm

As may be deduced from its name, the *Phoenix canariensis* illustrated is a native of the Canary Islands. It is hardier than the true date palm, *Phoenix dactylifera*. Both species are grown from pips, but it is a lengthy process. From May to July the plant must be fed every week.

Brown leaf-tips are generally caused by hard water, overwatering in winter or a dry soil-ball, which easily occurs where the root system has filled the pot. Yellow spots are due to insufficient light.

 Slight shade out of doors in summer; otherwise in a cool room

 Moderate (10–16°C (50–61°F) at night); keep frost-free in winter, preferably at 4°C (39°F)

 In summer give plenty of tepid, slightly demineralised water; in winter water sparingly

 Enjoys fresh air

 Prepacked potting compost

Phyllitis

Hart's tongue

This fern is indigenous in Europe and in North America. It is an evergreen, winterhardy plant, with undivided, shiny leathery leaves. Some varieties have strongly crispate or crinkly foliage; others have divided leaves. The spores appear in bands parallel to the lateral veins.

The best known species is *Phyllitis scolopendrium*, of which the garden form 'Undulata' is illustrated; this is a strain with wavy-edged foliage. Propagation is by sowing, by division or from lower stem cuttings rooted in bottom heat.

 Satisfied with very little light; may be grown indoors or out of doors

 Cold (3–10°C (37–50°F) at night); cool but frost-free in winter

 Water regularly, keeping the soil moist

 Fresh to humid air

 Humusy, calcareous potting compost

Pilea

Artillery plant

The *Pilea* owes its popular name to the fact that, when a flowering plant is sprayed, the filaments stretch and the pollen is forcefully ejected. Representatives of the more than four hundred evergreen and hardy species of this genus may be found in tropical regions all over the world.

The plants are propagated from shoots rooted in water, or in a mixture of equal parts of peat and sand, under glass and in bottom heat. The best time to take cuttings is in May; plants that have lost foliage are cut back in March–April. Pot and re-pot in a mixture consisting of, for instance, 2 parts leafmould, 2 parts rotted cow manure and 1 part rotted turves. Put a crock in the bottom of the pot. They can also be grown from seed.

From June to September give a dose of liquid fertiliser every week.

The best known *Pilea* species comes from Vietnam; this is *Pilea cadierei*, which has green leaves with silvery blotches between the veins. The insignificant white flowers appear in the leaf axils in spring and summer.

Pilea involucrata (upper photograph) has oval, deeply wrinkled green and dark brown leaves and plumes of white flowers. *Pilea microphylla*, with its tiny opposite-growing leaves, makes useful groundcover. This moss-like plant originates in South America; the little flowers grow in clumps in the axils. *Pilea nummulariifolia* has small circular leaves on creeping or trailing stems.

Pilea spruceana has hairy, wrinkled foliage; between the wrinkles the surface is quilted. The upper surface is bronze-green, the reverse is purple. The beautiful 'Norfolk' strain (lower photograph) has silver stripes between the veins.

☼   A well-lit situation, but out of direct bright sunlight

🌡   Warm or moderate (16–20°C (61–68°F) or 10–16°C (50–61°F) at night); 10–18°C (50–64°F) in winter

💧   In the growing period keep moderately moist; in winter give a little less water

   Moderate humidity

   Pre-packed potting compost

144

Piper

Pepper

There are about seven hundred pepper species, the best known being *Piper nigrum*, which provides us with black peppercorns. It may be used as a hanging or climbing house plant. The leaves are leathery, dark green, about 10cm (4in) in length, oval and sharply pointed. Keep cooler in winter. *Piper betle* (illustrated) is used in the tropics for the manufacture of sirih (betal). This plant may also be grown indoors. The finest foliage, with very delicate white and pink marking on a deep green background, is produced by *Piper ornatum*. In view of its need of humidity this species is best grown in a greenhouse. Propagation is from cuttings.

☼	May be grown in a well-lit, as well as in a fairly dark, position; does not tolerate full sun
🌡	Warm (16–20°C (61–68°F) at night); a little cooler in winter: about 14°C (57°F)
◊	Maintain constant moisture, but never too wet
⚞	Likes a high degree of humidity
⬟	Light, slightly acid soil

Pisonia

The plant in the photograph is often taken for a *Ficus*, but its name is *Pisonia brunoniana* or *Heimerliodendron brunonianum*. It requires approximately the same treatment as the *Ficus*; that is, to be kept in a warm room throughout the year. It does, however, require a fair amount of light since the variegated foliage contains little chlorophyll. Although there is of course an all-green—probably more resistant—form it is the variegated strain 'Variegata' which is usually seen. It is intolerant of excessively dry air.

Propagation is from cuttings, which root at 22°C (72°F)

☼	Requires fairly good light, but must be protected from full sun
🌡	Warm (16–20°C (61–68°F) at night); fairly warm in winter as well (18–20°C (64–68°F))
◊	The soil must be kept constantly, but moderately, moist
⚞	Fairly high degree of humidity
⬟	Nutritious mixture, rich in humus; for instance, 3 parts clay and 1 part leafmould

Pittosporum

A *Pittosporum* may grow into quite a shrub. Its vigorous, leathery foliage makes it appear that it would be a suitable plant for a warm room, but this is deceptive, for in winter it should have a cool environment and in summer it should, if possible, be put out of doors: in other words, it is suitable for use in a cool corridor or in tubs. I have several of these plants; in winter they live in a cool greenhouse at a minimum temperature of 5°C (41°F). The species seen most often is *Pittosporum tobira*, which has spoon-shaped leaves. There is also a variegated form 'Variegata' (photograph). The fragrant white flowers appear from May onwards.

☼ Out of doors in summer; stands up to sunlight; plenty of light throughout the year

🌡 Cold (3–10°C (37–50°F) at night); in winter keep cool as well (4–8°C (39–46°F))

💧 Water moderately; freely in sunny conditions

🌬 Likes fresh air

🪣 Somewhat chalky mixture

Platycerium

Stag's horn fern

There was a time when everyone wanted to possess a hart's horn fern, but now I get the impression that florists simply cannot get rid of them. Whether in fashion or not, they are most reliable and decorative plants, which have proved to be extremely resistant to the dry atmosphere of a living-room. This is chiefly due to the layer of wax which visibly covers the foliage. Once a houseproud owner removes this layer as being 'dirty' the plant will rapidly dry out.

The hart's horn is best grown in a special pot, hanging against a wall, with a saucer to collect the drips. A basket looks even better, but in that case you must take precautions to avoid your furniture being damaged by dripping water.

Make a habit of taking down the plant every week, plunging it in a large basin, so that the moss and fernroots can soak up plenty of water. Dissolve some dried cow manure or

Platycerium (continued)

other fertiliser in the water, for ferns like plenty of nourishment.

The best known and strongest species is *Platycerium bifurcatum*, also called *Platycerium alcicorne*. This plant is shown in both the photographs. You will see that the fern develops two kinds of foliage. The large, antler-shaped leaves are fertile and in maturity bear black spores on the underside. The inner leaves, initially green (photograph p. 146), conceal the centre of the plant. They subsequently turn brown (photograph on this page) and start to rot. They then feed the roots, but it is nevertheless advisable to use a fertiliser.

 Light to semi-shade; never in full sun

 Warm (16–20°C (61–68°F) at night); fairly warm in winter also (15°C (59°F)) minimum

 Keep the soil-ball constantly moist, preferably by plunging; a little drier in winter

 Moderate humidity is sufficient

 Special fern mixture, composed of sphagnum, fern roots and leafmould

Plectranthus

Various properties are ascribed to these simple little plants; they are, for instance, thought to keep rheumatism and moths at bay, but neither has been scientifically proved. Nevertheless there are people who swear by the *Plectranthus*, usually the species *Plectranthus fruticosus*, the larger plant in the photograph. Occasionally it puts forth small blue flowers, showing that it is related to the *Coleus*. The smaller plant is called *Plectranthus oertendahlii*; this species requires a higher degree of humidity. The plant is very easily increased from cuttings; it is advisable to do this every year

 Good light, but not in bright sunlight

 Moderate (10–16°C (50–61°F) at night); temperature in winter between 12 and 18°C (54–64°F)

 Water regularly and plentifully; after flowering keep a little drier

 Fairly resistant to dry living-room air

 Normal potting compost, to which a little extra peat may be added

147

Plumbago

Leadwort

Although this profusely flowering climber looks fairly delicate, it may be placed out of doors from the end of May onwards. At first it will not react very enthusiastically, but as soon as the sun gains in power flowerbuds will start to form and in summer numerous flowers of a magnificent sky-blue will open. Originally its name was *Plumbago capensis*, but it is now called *Plumbago auriculata* (photograph).

Propagation is from cuttings in autumn or spring; they root at 20–25°C (68–77°F).

☼	In summer a sunny spot out of doors; in the dormant season a well-lit position indoors
🌡	Moderate (10–16°C (50–61°F) at night); a little warmer is acceptable. 5–8°C (41–46°F) in the dormant season
◊	Freely in the growing and flowering seasons; in winter just enough to prevent drying out
☷	Moderate humidity
⬛	Nutritious, calcareous mixture

Polyscias

These fine, but rather difficult, foliage plants belong to the Aralia family, which is obvious from the junction between leafstalks and stem: very similar to that in the well-known garden shrub Aralia: compare also *Dizygotheca*, *Fatsia*, etc. In this plant, too, the long stalks bear grouped leaves; these are very decorative in the case of the species illustrated. The photograph on this page shows *Polyscias balfouriana*, a species with three unusual, shell-shaped leaves to each stalk. The colour is a beautiful green with white margins. In the cultivar 'Peacockii' the veins are white.

Polyscias filicifolia has 9–13 small, pale green leaves to each stalk; sometimes each leaf is subdivided. The shapes vary considerably.

In its native India *Polyscias fruticosa* grows to a 2–3m (6–10ft) tall shrub with 20–25cm (8–10in) doubly or trebly pinnate leaves. Stalks and veins are mottled. The small leaves are subdivided or serrated. Various strains of this species exist.

The beautiful foliage plant illustrated on this page is *Polyscias guilfoylei*. Each leafstalk bears

148

Polyscias (continued)

5–7 white-edged little leaves, all beautifully incised. The photograph shows a cutting, but mature plants may grow to at least 1m (40in) and will then have thousands of leaves. All the species mentioned are ideal for a greenhouse or a flower window. In the living-room the foliage will usually dry out, though I once saw a large specimen of *Polyscias balfouriana* growing in an office. The temperature should be 18 rather than 20°C (64°F, 68°F). Propagation is from cuttings rooted in spring in bottom heat, under glass.

 Shady situation

 Warm (16–20°C (61–68°F) at night); minimum temperature in winter 16°C (61°F)

 Requires plenty of moisture, preferably in the shape of tepid rainwater

 High degree of humidity, provided by frequent spraying and by the deep-plate method

 Loamy soil mixed with some sand and cow manure

Polystichum

Most species of this genus are known by the name of shield fern and grow wild in Europe. The best known form, suitable for greenhouse or indoor cultivation is *Polystichum tsussimense*, a fern with relatively firm, doubly-pinnate fronds, up to 20cm (8in) in length (photograph). Occasionally the holly fern, *Cyrtomium*, is classified as a *Polystichum*, but this is incorrect.

This is a stronger fern than most others because the foliage is leathery, so that transpiration is reduced. Nevertheless it is best combined with other plants in a container. Try to maintain a slightly lower temperature in winter. In summer feed often.

 Light to half-shady position

 Warm (16–20°C (61–68°F) at night); in winter keep at about 10°C (50°F)

 In summer give plenty of soft water; less in the cooler season

 Provide adequate humidity

 Normal pre-packed potting compost

Primula

Primulas are delightful indoor plants, true harbingers of spring. They are marketed at times varying from February to June; later-flowering plants are occasionally available as well. In theory some species can survive successfully over winter, but in practice this rarely works.

For prolonged enjoyment primulas should not be placed in too warm an environment. In a heated room they should at any rate be put close to the window, where it is usually a little cooler. Pay attention to watering: primulas are thirsty plants and it is advisable to use plastic pots from the start. *Primula vulgaris* may be put in a saucer constantly filled with water.

Another trick to obtain a prolonged flowering season is to give regular doses of a fertiliser solution. If the foliage turns yellow it means either that the plants are too dry, or that you have given so much fertiliser that the mineral concentration in the soil has become excessive. The latter may also be due to unsuitable water. Mineral poisoning may be cured by immediate re-potting.

The upper photograph shows *Primula malacoides*, in which the flowers grow round the stem at several levels; this is probably the most beautiful of the indoor species. Flowers are pink or white; the foliage and the stems are covered in a white farina. As a rule this plant is grown as an annual, but you may try to bring it through the winter by putting it in the garden in summer; do not set your expectations too high!

Primula obconica (lower photograph) has flowers growing in spherical umbels and large, hairy leaves. Some hairs secrete a substance called primine to which certain people are allergic; it causes skin irritation and sometimes even a rash. There are now strains on the market in which this substance is lacking, but unfortunately the fact is never mentioned on the label. The flowers occur in red, rose-red, blue and white. These plants tolerate a warmer situation than the previous species and they can overwinter in the garden or in a cold frame. Re-pot after flowering.

In Switzerland new strains are being cultivated in the colours red, blue, bright yellow, golden-orange, etc. These novelties make hardier pot-plants than *Primula vulgaris*; they are

Primula (continued)

called *Primula polyantha* 'Niederlenz'.

The adjoining photograph shows two examples of *Primula praenitens*, better known as *Primula sinensis*. It occurs in numerous colours and is occasionally available in full flower in October. Reasonably resistant to dry living-room air, it also requires slightly less water.

Primula vulgaris with its bright colours (its former name, now obsolete, was *Primula acaulis*) is actually a garden species; it is found on the market from February onwards. It is very intolerant of high temperatures.

All species can be grown from seed, in a cool position.

☼ Never in the sun; always put in a half-shady position; outside in summer

🌡 Fairly cool (5–10°C (41–50°F) at night); in winter keep at 12°C (54°F)

💧 Keep very moist, using tepid, slightly demineralised water; give even more water in the flowering period

≋ Moderate humidity

▽ Compost-based potting soil

Pseuderanthemum

This is a typical foliage plant with very dark leaves, known also as *Eranthemum*. The species illustrated is *Pseuderanthemum atropurpureum*. The wine-red leaves are frequently spotted with olive-green. In addition to brown-leaved species there are also green, golden-veined forms.

This is a suitable plant for the greenhouse or the flower window. In the living-room the air is too dry. Older plants soon become unsightly and it is therefore advisable regularly to take cuttings which will root at a bottom heat of 25°C (77°F); the young plants must be cultivated in the greenhouse.

☼ Slight shade is best

🌡 Warm (16–20°C (61–68°F) at night); in winter 16–18°C (61–64°F)

💧 In the growing period the soil-ball should be kept moist with soft water; in winter keep a little drier

≋ High degree of humidity; spray often

▽ Normal potting compost

Pseudomammillaria

In many books this plant is found under the name *Dolichothele*. However, the species illustrated has differently shaped flowers; its official name is *Pseudomammillaria camptotricha*.

This cactus grows readily in any kind of soil and puts forth a large number of shoots. The long spines of the individual globes intertwine, creating an extremely entangled mass. The brown and green colours go well together.

In summer place the plant in very good light; in winter it must be kept cool and dry, or it will die.

As much light and sun as possible

Warm (16–20°C (61–67°F) at night); in winter a temperature of 6–12°C (43–54°F)

In the growing period it should not be too dry; water from the bottom. Give hardly any water in winter

Low humidity

Standard potting compost or a special cactus mixture

Pteris

Ribbon fern

The *Pteris* genus comprises some of the best known and most popular fern species. They possess scaly rhizomes and single-, sometimes double-pinnate, feathery fronds. There are about three hundred species with widely varying, unusually shaped foliage, generally green, although some strains have white-striped leaves. The spores grow along the margins of the leaves, except at the tip. Propagation is from ripe spores, which germinate in damp peat at 25°C (77°F). The plants are then cultivated in a moderate temperature. Increase by division is also possible.

Pteris cretica is the species best known as a house plant. As a rule the foliage is pale green and slightly leathery. The adjoining photograph shows the strain 'Albolineata' (left), with a creamy stripe down the leaves. Other forms grown on a large scale are 'Major', 'Wimsettii' and 'Wilsonii' (photograph on p. 153). Two white variegated strains of *Pteris ensiformis* are in cultivation: 'Evergemiensis'

Pteris (continued)

and 'Victoriae' (photograph this page, right).

Pteris multifida resembles *Pteris cretica*, but has very narrow leaves. *Pteris quadriaurita* has double- or treble-pinnate fronds with sessile side leaves, sometimes silver-striped. *Pteris tremula* is another well-known house plant.

All species should be fed every week, for ferns adore fertiliser. They detest hard water.

☼ Always a half-shady position

🌡 Moderate (10–16°C (50–61°F) at night); variegated strains 10–12°C (50–54°F), green-leaved forms 16–18°C (61–64°F) in winter

💧 In the growing season water freely, using soft, tepid water; give less in winter, but do not keep too dry

💨 Maintain a high degree of humidity

🪣 Mixture of potting compost and beech leaves

Punica

Pomegranate

The pomegranate is a deciduous, thorny shrub which has been in cultivation since time immemorial. It originated in North Africa, from where it spread to Persia and India.

The terminal growing flowers have an orange-red corolla; the edge of the petals is fleshy. Flowering occurs from June to September. The fruits of *Punica granatum* illustrated do not ripen in all areas; they drop, together with the foliage, at the first sign of nightfrost.

New plants may be grown from seed in March, or from cuttings rooted in bottom heat.

☼ In summer a sunny outdoor spot is preferred, but it can remain indoors

🌡 Moderate (10–16°C (50–61°F) at night); keep at 4–6°C (39–43°F) in winter until new growth appears

💧 In the growing period keep moderately moist; water sparingly from August onwards

💨 Likes fresh, moderately humid air

🪣 Compost-based potting soil

Rebutia

This is a genus of small spherical cacti. The flowers appear—sometimes at an early age—at the base of the globes and are often very large in proportion to the body of the plant. Propagation is by division or from seed, which should be covered with a little sand. From April to June give a cactus fertiliser; in summer provide adequate fresh air.

The plant illustrated is *Rebutia miniscula*. Other well-known species are: *Rebutia chrysacantha*, with red flowers and golden-yellow spines; *Rebutia marsoneri*, *Rebutia senilis* and *Rebutia xanthocarpa*.

☼ Fairly sunny position in summer; good light in the dormant season

🌡 Moderate to warm (13–18°C (55–64°F) at night); 6–8°C (43–46°F) in winter

💧 Water fairly freely in summer, then gradually decrease; keep dry in winter

💨 Stands up well to dry living-room air

🪣 Special cactus mixture

Rechsteineria

The soft-haired *Rechsteineria cardinalis* (photograph) is a native of Brazil. The tubular red flowers grow horizontally. Propagation is from seed, from leaf-cuttings or from shoots, preferably with a section of tuber attached. Fully grown plants should be fed every fortnight from May to September. In winter the tubers are kept at a minimum temperature of 12°C (54°F). In February they are planted in damp peat or fresh soil, eyes just emerging, and brought into growth at 21°C (70°F).

☼ Half-shady situation

🌡 Warm (16–20°C (61–68°F) at night); tubers are kept at 12–15°C (54–59°F) in winter; bring into growth at about 20°C (68°F)

💧 In the flowering period water normally, using soft water; then gradually decrease until the foliage dies back

💨 High degree of humidity

🪣 Well-drained soil, rich in humus. Keep the tubers dry in the pot-soil in winter

Rhaphidophora

At one time this plant was erroneously called *Scindapsus* but, when the discrepancies in the inflorescence were discovered, the plant illustrated was included in the *Rhaphidophora* genus. The leaves of *Rhaphidophora aurea* (photograph) are heart-shaped with an asymmetrical tip; they are striped or blotched with yellow. It is a vigorous climber, which attaches itself by its aerial roots. The 'Marble Queen' strain contains very little chlorophyll and is consequently very slow-growing.

Propagation is from severed runners or stem-sections with 1–2 leaf-buds and aerial roots. The soil mixture should contain peat and sphagnum.

☼ Variegated forms require more light than green species, which will survive in deep shade

🌡 Warm (16–20°C (61–68°F) at night); in winter the temperature must not drop below 16°C (61°F)

💧 Water moderately

💨 Resistant to dry living-room air

🪣 Standard to slightly acid mixture

Rhipsalidopsis

Rhipsalidopsis gaertneri (photograph) is a strongly branching cactus with curving stems; the lower joints are triangular to hexagonal; the upper, younger sections are flat. The flowers are scarlet with slightly outcurving, pointed petals.

The somewhat rarer species *Rhipsalidopsis rosea* has fragrant pink flowers.

Propagation from seed or from tip cuttings, which must be left to dry out first. When the first buds appear, increase the water supply and from now on do not move or turn the plant, as this increases the risk of the buds dropping.

☼ From June onwards a shady position out of doors. Light shade indoors

🌡 Warm (16–20°C (61–68°F) at night); from September onwards keep in a cool spot; 5–10°C (41–50°F) in January–February until the buds begin to form

💧 Keep the soil-ball moist; fairly dry before flowering

💨 Moderate humidity

🪣 Standard potting compost

Rhoeo

Rhoeo has elongated leaves, growing in funnel-shaped rosettes. The upper surface is green or has pale longitudinal stripes (for instance in *Rhoeo spathacea*, photograph); the reverse is purple. The small white flowers, surrounded by shell-shaped bracts, appear in the axils of the lower leaves.

Propagation from seed or from shoots, which will root readily in sandy soil, after which they are potted in a friable mixture rich in humus. From March until August feed every week.

☼ Half-shady position; the variegated form requires a little more light, but no direct sunlight

🌡 Moderate (10–16°C (50–61°F) at night); in winter a minimum of 10°C (50°F)

💧 In summer water freely with soft, tepid water; keep drier in the dormant season

🌫 Requires a humid atmosphere

🪣 Standard potting compost

Rhoicissus

This genus comprises twelve evergreen climbing species. The best known is *Rhoicissus capensis* (photograph), which has undivided leaves covered in brown hairs in the early stages.

Remember that this plant needs a cool position, for instance in the hall.

Re-pot every year in April in porous, chalky soil. From May to September feed once a fortnight. Occasionally sponge the leaves.

Propagation from shoots, rooted at 16–18°C (61–64°F) in a mixture of peat and sand. Stem-sections with at least two nodes may also be used.

See also under *Cissus*.

☼ Half- to deep shade

🌡 Cool to moderate (8–14°C (46–57°F) at night); 6–10°C (43–50°F) in winter

💧 Water moderately, even less in the cooler winter season

🌫 Not very tolerant of dry air; spray from time to time

🪣 Chalky mixture

Rochea

Of the species originating in South Africa, the *Rochea coccinea* (illustrated) is the one to be recommended most. This succulent shrub-like plant has been used as a house plant for quite some time; it stands out because of its scarlet flower umbels, which appear in June. The erect growing stems are densely covered in opposite pairs of leaves.

Propagation is from cuttings in March—the cut surface must first dry out—or from seed, which will germinate in about a fortnight. The seeds remain germinant for two years. Seedlings are potted in loamy, sandy soil in fairly small pots.

 In summer it may be put out of doors; protect from bright sunlight; good light in the dormant season

 Cold to moderate (5–12°C (41–54°F) at night); allow a dormant season at 4–8°C (39–46°F)

 In summer water adequately; keep drier during the rest of the year

 Enjoys fresh, slightly humid air

Slightly calcareous mixture

Rosa

Rose

The 'Happy' strain illustrated is one of the miniature roses cultivated in the Netherlands; they flower profusely from March to October, although they do not grow beyond 20–30cm (8–12in). To make these roses flower in winter they are forced. Faded blooms must be removed immediately, since rose-hips, if allowed to develop, take too much of the plant's strength. The 'Happy' rose illustrated is semi-double, as is 'Doc', which has slightly larger flowers. 'Sleepy' is a double pink rose.

Propagation is quite difficult and is best left to the professional.

 Light, sunny situation

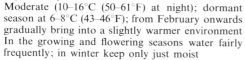 Moderate (10–16°C (50–61°F) at night); dormant season at 6–8°C (43–46°F); from February onwards gradually bring into a slightly warmer environment

 In the growing and flowering seasons water fairly frequently; in winter keep only just moist

 Humidity required, especially in spring

Use a proprietary potting compost

Saintpaulia

African violet

This very well known little plant originates in the jungle of the Usambara mountains in East Africa. It is a low-growing herbaceous plant with leaves growing in rosettes. The leaves are rounded-oval, fleshy, usually dark green and covered in vertical hairs of approximately equal length. The flowers grow in the axils in multi-flowered clusters. African violets may flower profusely at almost any time of the year.

As a result of crossing or of ray treatment, numerous strains have been developed in addition to the original violet-blue species. They vary in the colour of the flowers as well as in that of the foliage; they may be single or double and have crisped or wavy leaf-edges. Apart from *Saintpaulia ionantha* (photographs), we also know *Saintpaulia confusa*, which has oblong leaves with recumbent hairs of unequal length. The fruits are oblong, while those of *Saintpaulia ionantha* are spherical.

The plants may be grown from seed sown in late January in a bottom heat 20°C (68°F), but it is much easier to grow them from leaf-cuttings. Mature leaves with a section of stalk are inserted upright in a mixture of peat fibre and sand and are rooted in a temperature of 20°C (68°F). Roots will also develop in a bottle of water. Young plants are potted in wide bowls.

In the flowering season feed regularly. When watering be careful to avoid drops on the leaves, as this will cause staining. After flowering water a little less and give the plant a short rest. Soon new flower-buds will appear.

When the pot becomes too small, the plants must be re-potted, preferably in a shallow, wide pot or bowl, so that the leaves hang above the soil; the plants will thus suffer less from dry air.

In summer a slightly shady position; in winter good light, but out of the sun

Moderate to warm (13–18°C (55–64°F) at night); 15–18°C (59–64°F) in the resting period

In the growing and flowering seasons keep constantly moist using tepid, soft water

Intolerant of dry air

Slightly humusy mixture; proprietary potting compost

158

Sansevieria

Mother-in-law's tongue

This plant made its way into our living-rooms in about 1930 and since then has never lost its popularity. This may be explained by the fact that its somewhat succulent nature makes it resistant to temporary neglect, while its tolerance of dry air is another advantage. Almost the only ways to kill a *Sansevieria* are overwatering or giving it too cold a spot.

Most species originate in tropical regions of South Africa, where *Sansevieria cylindrica* is still being used as raw material in the production of fibres. In the background, right, you see *Sansevieria trifasciata*, which has dull-green, erect, lancet-shaped leaves, cross-banded in paler green. To the left the very well-known form 'Laurentii', in which the leaves have a golden yellow margin.

'Hahnii' (foreground, left) is low-growing and forms funnel-shaped rosettes. 'Golden Hahnii' (foreground, right) has yellow bands along the margins. There is also a 'Silver Hahnii', with white banding. All these small *trifasciata* forms are slightly more tender than their larger counterparts. They must not be kept too moist, require a resting period in winter, and their position must be neither too well lit nor too dark. *Sansevieria longiflora* is not very well known; this is a pity, for it has a striking inflorescence and beautifully marbled, dark green foliage. At the back of the pot in the left foreground you see *Sansevieria senegambica*, which has grey-green leaves, sometimes faintly striped along the edges.

The plants are best increased by division. They may also be grown from leaf-cuttings, but this requires a high bottom temperature. It must also be remembered that cuttings taken from variegated forms will revert to green, since it is the green parts of the leaf that strike root. Pot in chalky soil.

☼ No special requirements, but bright sunlight will affect the foliage marking

🌡 Warm (16–20°C (61–68°F) at night); minimum temperature in winter 13°C (55°F)

◊ Water moderately; in winter keep fairly dry. Give nitrogen-free fertiliser

≋ Stands up well to dry air

⊔ Coarse, slightly alkaline soil

Saxifraga

Mother-of-thousands

Saxifraga stolonifera is a rosette-forming little plant, whose waterfall of runners makes it very suitable for use as a hanging plant. In this species the foliage is dull green with white veins, red on the reverse; in the 'Tricolor' strain (photograph) the leaves are more deeply incised, have a white margin and irregular white and red mottling. In spring and summer it produces 20–40cm (8–16in) long plumes of small white or pink flowers. The strain grows slowly, flowers less profusely and requires a higher temperature than the species. In the growing period feed every fortnight.

Propagation by rooting the runners.

☼	Requires plenty of light, but no direct sun
🌡	Moderate (10–16°C (50–61°F) at night); in the dormant season maintain a temperature of 10–12°C (50–54°F)
💧	The soil-ball must be kept moist. Beware of overwatering, especially in winter
💨	Moderate humidity
🪣	Pre-packed potting compost

Schefflera

In its native Australia *Schefflera* is an evergreen tree, growing to 40m (130ft) in height and bearing long-stalked, oblong and leathery leaves in groups of three or more. In summer it produces magnificent red flowers, but these will, unfortunately never be seen in the living room. The photograph shows *Schefflera digitata*, which requires a slightly higher temperature than *Schefflera actinophylla* with its somewhat thicker leaves.

In summer it should be given a well-lit and airy situation, but out of the sun and especially out of any draught. It may also be put in a sheltered position out of doors.

Propagation is from fresh, imported seed.

☼	Plenty of light and space throughout the year; tolerates a fair amount of shade
🌡	Moderate (10–16°C (50–61°F) at night); temperature in winter 12–16°C (54–61°F). May be placed outside in summer
💧	Water moderately; keep fairly dry in the dormant season
💨	Moderate humidity
🪣	Compost-based potting soil; provide good drainage

Scindapsus

The *Scindapsus* genus, which originates in south-eastern Asia, now contains only one species: *Scindapsus pictus* (illustrated). It is a climber with thick leaves, on the upper surface dark green with blue-green and cream spots. The 'Argyraeus' strain has smaller leaves with clearer white marking and a silvery margin; it is a little more sensitive than the main species and likes to be kept in a tropical plant window. It is fairly easy to propagate from cuttings; the new plant is transferred to a well-drained pot in potting compost to which some peat, sand and sphagnum have been added.

See also under *Rhapsidophora*.

☼ A well-lit situation out of the sun; tolerates shade

🌡 Warm (16–20°C (61–68°F) at night); requires a fairly high temperature in winter also

💧 Water moderately but regularly throughout the year, using tepid water

💨 Requires a high degree of humidity

🪴 Well-drained soil, for instance potting compost mixed with sand, sphagnum and peat

Scirpus

Club rush

This graceful, grass-like little plant grows to 25–30cm (10–12in). Its bright green, needle-fine leaves initially grow erect; they later curve downwards, so that the plant may be used as a hanging plant. In summer little spikes of white flowers are developed at the extremities of the blades; they look like bits of fluff.

To keep *Scirpus cernuus* (illustrated) in good condition, the soil must be kept constantly wet; this is best achieved by placing the pot in a saucer of water.

Propagation is by division.

☼ Half-shady position

🌡 Moderate to warm (13–18°C (55–64°F) at night) throughout the year

💧 Water very generously; there must always be water in the saucer

💨 High degree of humidity

🪴 Pot in nutritious, loamy soil, in pots with saucer attached

Sedum

Stonecrop

This genus embraces six hundred species, including winterhardy plants from colder regions. We shall deal only with a number of species suitable for indoor cultivation.

Sedum dendroideum (photograph, background, right) develops an irregularly branching little trunk with fairly thick, circular to spoon-shaped waxy leaves and a flower-stalk bearing star-shaped yellow flowers. The species is a native of Mexico, as is *Sedum humifusum*, a low-growing plant with yellow flowers, illustrated in the foreground, left. *Sedum rubrotinctum* (foreground, right) is a very well-known red succulent which grows to only 20cm (8in). The cylindrical leaves, growing on slender stalks, break off easily and root themselves. As a rule the stalks are recumbent at first, but later grow erect. The flowers are yellow.

In the background (left) you see *Sedum sieboldii*, a native of Japan, which produces pink flower umbels in the autumn. The leaves are blue-green, edged in red; they always grow in threes at intervals of more than 1cm ($\frac{2}{5}$in). This is a winterhardy species which fades in the autumn. There is a variegated strain called 'Mediovariegatum'. Grow in very sandy soil.

Sedum bellum is a creamy-white, winter-flowering hanging plant. *Sedum pachyphyllum* is erect-growing; its circular leaves are tipped with red. Another form not illustrated is *Sedum morganianum*, a very unusual species with drooping stems bearing cylindrical pointed leaves, perfectly aligned. *Sedum stahlii* has bean-shaped leaves on erect growing stems.

The plants can be increased from stem- or leaf-cuttings. The cut surfaces must be left to dry before they are inserted in a mixture of sand and peat. Can also be grown from seed.

It is advisable never to feed a *Sedum.* Excessive watering causes decay.

☼ A well-lit, sunny spot; in summer it may be placed in a sheltered outdoor position

🌡 Moderate (10–16°C (50–61°F) at night); keep cool in winter at 7–10°C (45–50°F), in good light

💧 Water moderately in summer, keep fairly dry in winter

Reasonably resistant to dry air

🪣 Nutritious sandy and humusy soil

Selaginella

Creeping moss

There are seven hundred different *Selaginella* species. Most of these originate in tropical rain forests, but there are a number of low-growing species from more temperate regions, which must consequently be grown in a cooler environment (day temperature 5–20°C (41–68°F)); one of these is *Selaginella apoda*. The minimum temperature for taller growing species, including *Selaginella martensii* (illustrated) is 12°C (54°F).

Propagation is by division, or from tip-cuttings rooted in bottom heat. The cuttings should occasionally be sprayed. Fertiliser should be greatly diluted.

☼ Very tolerant of shade

🌡 Moderate to warm (10–20°C (50–68°F)), depending on the species

💧 Water moderately, using soft water; never allow to dry out

༄ Fresh, humid air

🪴 Friable, nutritious soil, in shallow, well-drained pots

Selenicereus

Night cactus

This cactus has blue-green, limp and trailing stems, about 2–3cm ($\frac{3}{4}$–$1\frac{1}{4}$in) thick. The shoots sometimes grow to 1.5m (5ft); it is therefore advisable to train the plant against a trellis. As the popular name indicates, *Selenicereus grandiflorus* flowers at night (in summer). Towards 3pm the buds begin to swell and by 10pm the flower is fully open. By about midnight it has closed again and the following morning an insignificant, limp relic is all that remains of the wonderful spectacle.

Propagation from cuttings or from seed.

☼ In summer a well-lit position out of direct sunlight; plenty of light in winter

🌡 Moderate to warm (14–18°C (57–64°F) at night); keep at 10–20°C (50–68°F) in winter

💧 In summer keep fairly moist; spray until it flowers. In winter water sparingly

༄ Enjoys fresh air

🪴 Light soil, rich in humus

Sempervivum

House leek

This is an undemanding little succulent, easily grown from seed or from detached rosettes.

The photograph shows (background, left) *Sempervivum tectorum* spp. *calcareum* 'Nigricans', with brown-tipped green foliage. In *Sempervivum arachnoideum* (left foreground) the rosettes appear to be covered in cobweb. This is one of the best known species. In the centre background you see *Sempervivum thompsonii*; in the background, right, is *Sempervivum tectorum*, with in front of it a strain of this species called 'Emerald'.

☼ Sunny, well-lit spot, in- or out of doors

🌡 Cold (3–10°C (37–50°F) at night); all *Sempervivum* species are winter-hardy

💧 Water sparingly throughout the year; very resistant to drought

💨 Low humidity adequate

🥣 Sandy mixture, poor in humus

Senecio

Cineraria

The plant in the adjoining photograph used to be sold under the name *Cineraria*, but its correct name is *Senecio cruentus*; the photograph shows one of its numerous hybrids. The plant is a native of the Canary Islands.

It is an annual; its flowering season may be prolonged to some extent by placing the plant in a cool position and giving it only tepid water.

Greenfly are usually the result of draught or of too warm a position. In the growing and flowering season give liquid fertiliser every fortnight.

Propagation is a job for the expert.

☼ A half-shady position

🌡 Cold (3–10°C (37–50°F) at night); during the day the temperature must not be too high either

💧 Water moderately to freely; keep the soil moist

💨 Enjoys fresh, slightly humid air, but never place it in a draught

🥣 Calcareous potting mixture

164

Senecio (Succulent Species)

The *Senecio* genus embraces a large number of succulent species which in no way resemble the *Senecio cruentus* described on the facing page. The leaves are fleshy and contain a great deal of sap; this keeps the plants alive in times of drought. They really are extremely easy succulents which can be killed only by over-watering. If you have a liberal hand when watering you would be well advised to use pots with holes, filling them halfway up with crocks, since otherwise the plants are bound to come to grief.

All species like plenty of light and a cool position in winter. Sometimes they produce flowers, but these are of minor importance. On the other hand the foliage can be extremely interesting; just consider the *Senecio herreianus* (in the upper photograph) with its spherical little leaves, like threaded peas. A very similar form is *Senecio citriformis*, with lemon-shaped leaves. *Senecio haworthii* has more pointed leaves. The last three species used to be called *Kleinia*.

In addition there are species with thick, cylindrical stems, such as the vigorous *Senecio articulatus* which, with its jointed stems and unusually incised leaves, looks like a plant from a horror film. Other species resemble *Echeveria* or *Crassula*. *Senecio stapeliiformis* has stems resembling those of the carrion flower, *Stapelia* (p. 171).

Odd man out is the German ivy, *Senecio mikanioides*. The thin but nevertheless fleshy foliage is remarkably similar to that of the ivy. It is a very vigorous hanging plant. Its variegated counterpart is even finer; this, however, is called *Senecio macroglossus* 'Variegatus' (lower photograph). Do not give it too dark a position.

All species are increased from cuttings, which will present no problem. Fleshy cuttings must first dry out.

☼ The best lit, sunniest position available

🌡 In winter a maximum of 12°C (54°F); in summer moderate (10–16°C (50–61°F) at night)

◊ In the dormant season (in summer) water very sparingly; give a little more in the growing period

  Moderate humidity

⬛ Sandy-loamy potting mixture, in shallow bowls

Setcreasea

The photograph shows *Setcreasea purpurea*, a purple plant growing to about 40cm (16in), after which the stems curve, so that it may be used as a hanging plant. The leaves are sessile, slightly hairy; the upper surface is blue-bloomed. The corolla of the flowers is pink.

New plants are grown in spring from young ground shoots; they root fairly easily in some degree of bottom heat.

In the growing season the plant should be fed from time to time but be very sparing with nitrogen.

☼   A well-lit and/or sunny position

🌡   Moderate to warm (13–18°C (55–64°F) at night); in winter the temperature may drop to freezing point

💧   Keep the soil-ball moderately moist; do not let it dry out; do not water on the foliage

≋   Moderate humidity

🪣   Slightly chalky mixture

Siderasis

This plant is related to the *Setcreasea* described above, as well as to the *Tradescantia*. *Siderasis fuscata* (photograph), a native of Brazil, is the sole species. The upper surface of the leaves is green, with a central white stripe and reddish-brown hairs; the reverse is red. Mature leaves are usually 20cm (8in) long and 8cm (3in) wide. The colour of the flowers varies from blue to red.

These plants are increased by division of mature plants.

From April to August they may be fed every 2–3 weeks with a weak solution.

☼   Shady situation

🌡   Warm (16–20°C (61–68°F) at night); a little cooler in winter

💧   Water regularly, keeping the soil moist

≋   Fairly high degree of humidity

🪣   Somewhat loamy potting mixture

166

Sinningia

Gloxinia

This plant has stalkless leaves, growing from tubers up to 3cm (1¼in) in diameter; mature leaves easily attain a size of 25 × 20cm (10 × 8in). The foliage is covered in velvety hairs and is occasionally reddish on the reverse. The flowers are long-stemmed and bell-shaped. The original species, a native of Brazil, had violet-coloured flowers. The form illustrated as a pink *Sinningia speciosa*. There are now hybrids in many different shades, often with a contrasting band to the petals. Propagation is from leaf-cuttings or from runners. Lack of humidity, excessively damp soil and cold water are all fatal to these plants.

☼ Well-lit position, out of the sun's rays

🌡 Warm (16–20°C (61–68°F) at night); keep the tubers dry at 6°C (43°F) in winter; bring them into growth at 18°C (64°F)

💧 Maintain constant moisture, using likewarm water containing 0.5 gram of fertiliser per litre (about 1/10 oz/gal)

💨 Moderate humidity

🪣 Proprietary potting compost with the addition of a little peat

Skimmia

This is a slow-growing, evergreen shrub, indigenous in cool but frostfree regions. The *Skimmia japonica* in the adjoining photograph comes from Japan. It flowers in May; the flowers are creamy-white and are followed by bright red berries which last for a long time.

As a rule *Skimmia* is dioecious; in other words, there are separate male (*S. fragrans*) and female (*S. oblata*) plants. To obtain berries you will therefore need both species. Out of doors, insects will look after the pollination but indoors you will have to deal with this yourself.

☼ A half-shady position indoors; may be placed outside in summer

🌡 Cold to moderate (5–12°C (41–54°F) at night); it is not winter-hardy

💧 Water moderately, using hand-hot water; make sure that the soil-ball does not dry out

💨 Enjoys a cool, well-ventilated environment

🪣 Slightly acid, well-draining mixture

Smithiantha

This genus comprises eight species, well worth growing both for their variety, multicoloured leaves and for their flowers. The inflorescence consists of a raceme of short-stalked, pendulous flowers, usually in shades of yellow, red or pink.

The members of the species are as a rule seen only in botanical gardens, but there are very fine hybrids for indoor cultivation, such as the one in the photograph.

At the end of the winter the rhizomes are brought into growth at a bottom heat of 22°C (72°F). Delay feeding until the shoots are 10cm (4in) in length.

☼ Well-lit position with a little diffused sunlight; no direct sun

🌡 Warm (16–20°C (61–68°F) at night); keep the root-stock at 10–12°C (50–54°F) in winter. When the plant is in flower the temperature may be slightly lower

💧 Water moderately, using tepid water

💨 High degree of humidity; do not let the foliage get wet

🪣 Standard pre-packed potting compost

Solanum

Christmas cherry

The photograph shows *Solanum pseudocapsicum* as it is found at the florists' in autumn or winter. It flowers in May–June, when the small white flowers clearly show the plant's relationship to the potato. In each flower-umbel only one flower is fertile. Artificial pollination increases the chance of fruits; these keep longest if the plant is given a cool situation. When the leaves have dropped the plant is pruned and given a rest; in March it will start into growth once more. Feed regularly in summer; it may be placed out of doors at this time, provided it is brought indoors before the first night frost.

☼ A sunny position; may stand outside in summer, but must be brought indoors in good time

🌡 Cold to moderate (7–11°C (45–52°F) at night); 8–10°C (46–50°F) in the autumn. *Solanum* is very sensitive to frost

💧 Water freely in the flowering period; afterwards less, but never let the plant dry out entirely

💨 Enjoys fresh, slightly humid air

🪣 Nutritious, somewhat loamy soil

Soleirolia

Soleirolia soleirolii is a low-growing, creeping plant, indigenous in Corsica and Sardinia; its other name is *Helxine*. It is very suitable for use under greenhouse staging, where the little plants with their recumbent, threadlike stalks form large green cushions. The scattered leaves, only about 5–10mm ($\frac{1}{5}$–$\frac{2}{5}$in) in size, are asymmetrical, heart- or kidney-shaped. The flowers, too, are minute; they are greenish in colour and grow in the axils of the leaves.

Propagation by division is very simple. As the plant grows very rapidly, you will in no time have one to give away as a present.

 Diffused sunlight or semi-shade; may be put outside in summer

 Moderate (10–16°C (50–61°F) at night); in winter possibly a little cooler

 Water freely in the growing period; keep moist in winter also

 Moderate to high degree of humidity

 Somewhat humusy potting compost

Sonerila

This genus includes about 175 species of tropical flowering plants, of which only *Sonerila margaritacea* (illustrated) is popular for use indoors. This very decorative little plant, a native of Java, is very suitable for inclusion in bottle gardens. It is a shrubby little plant with recumbent red stalks, bearing leaves that are shiny green on their upper surface. Silvery spots are arranged in lines between the lateral veins. The reverse is paler in colour, with purple veins. The flowers are bright pink. Take tip-cuttings in spring and root them in a bottom heat of 30°C (86°F); plant in shallow pots.

Semi-shade

Warm (16–20°C (61–68°F) at night); keep at 18°C (64°F) in winter

Water freely in the growing period; do not allow the plant to dry out in winter

Maintain a fairly high degree of humidity

Friable, humusy mixture, containing plenty of leaf-mould (beech leaves)

Sparmannia

House lime

This relative of the lime tree may grow into an enormous plant in the living-room, but may be held in check to some extent. The *Sparmannia africana* illustrated, for instance, may be pruned after flowering; this is best done at the end of the resting period, which takes place in May. The large, heart-shaped leaves are pale green and felty. The white flowers appear in umbels and have numerous stamens. Propagation is from flower-shoots in spring. Ensure adequate bottom heat.

 Well-lit, sunny and airy position. Do not place too close to other plants

Moderate (10–16°C (50–61°F) at night); in the dormant season, from October to December, 6–10°C (43–50°F)

Water freely in the growing season, a little less in winter. Do not let the plant dry out

 Reasonably tolerant of dry air

Standard pre-packed potting compost

Spathiphyllum

Peace lily

This plant prefers the shady, warm and humid environment of a hothouse but, provided you ensure adequate humidity (for instance by means of the deep-plate method), it may be brought indoors for a short period when it is in flower.

The inflorescence of *Spathiphyllum wallisii* (photograph) shows clearly that it is a member of the Arum lily family.

The plant is easily increased by division or from seed. In the growing period feed at most once a fortnight. Re-pot in February–March; provide good drainage.

 Fair amount of shade accepted

Warm (16–20°C (61–68°F) at night); minimum temperature in winter 14–16°C (57–61°F)

Water regularly and fairly freely in the growing period; a little less in winter

 High degree of humidity

 Friable mixture containing plenty of sphagnum

Stapelia

Carrion flower

The photograph shows *Stapelia variegata*, which flowers from August to October. The flowers have a most disagreeable smell; hence the common name.

Stapelia species are fairly easily grown succulents. It is important that they are kept cool in winter and are then watered only just sufficiently to prevent them shrivelling up. Excess watering will cause the stems to decay.

Propagation is reasonably easy; stem cuttings are set in sand after the cut surfaces have been left to dry. Plant in well-draining pots.

☼ A sunny spot in summer; best possible light in winter

🌡 Moderate to warm (13–18°C (55–64°F) at night); keep cool in winter

◊ Keep fairly dry, especially in the dormant season

〰 Very tolerant of dry air

🪣 Mix 2 parts leafmould with 1 part sand, adding a little loam and chalk

Stenandrium

Of the thirty species belonging to this genus only one is in cultivation, namely *Stenandrium lindenii* (photograph). This low-growing, shrubby little plant comes from Peru. The stalks are very short, the leaves are blistered and oval in shape; the upper surface is dark green with yellow veining; the reverse is reddish in colour. The flower spikes produce small yellow flowers. This is an excellent plant for providing ground cover in plant containers.

A constant temperature of 20–22°C (68–72°F) is essential to keep the plant in fine and healthy condition. Shoots are rooted in a bottom heat of 30°C (86°F).

☼ Light shade

🌡 Warm (16–20°C (61–68°F) at night); keep the daytime temperature at about 20°C (68°F) throughout the year

◊ Keep constantly moist

〰 High degree of humidity required; spray often

🪣 Proprietary potting compost mixed with some leafmould; pot in shallow bowls

Stenotaphrum

In tropical and sub-tropical countries this grass species is occasionally used for lawns. Wild species usually occur along the coastline. The form used as a house plant is *Stenotaphrum secundatum*, and more particularly the 'Variegatum' strain illustrated; this has creamy longitudinal stripes on the ribbon-shaped leaves. Both in the species and in the strain roots grow from the nodes and young plants are developed which may be potted separately. *Stenotaphrum* can also be propagated from stem cuttings; several of these are combined in a pot to achieve bushy growth.

 A sunny situation

 Moderate to warm (13–18°C (55–64°F) at night); a little cooler in winter

 Water moderately

 Moderate humidity; likes fresh air

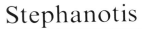 Proprietary potting compost with a little pulverised loam or clay

Stephanotis

Of the five species of this genus, originating in Madagascar, only *Stephanotis floribunda*, the Madagascar jasmine, is in cultivation. A deliciously scented flowering specimen is a real ornament in your home. It has added significance, for the flowers—a detail is illustrated—are frequently used in bridal sprays.

In the living-room *Stephanotis* is best trained on a trellis or on bent wire. To maintain adequate humidity the foliage should be sprayed from time to time. Give a dose of liquid fertiliser every fortnight from May to September.

The best time to re-pot is in April, at first annually, later once every three years. An attack of scaly or mealy bug is frequently the result of too high a temperature in winter. Check constantly, and once a month spray with a mixture of soap and methylated spirits.

In a warm, or better still, a moderate greenhouse (minimum temperature in winter 12°C (54°F)) *Stephanotis* may be trained over a large area of the glass. In the flowering season it is a ravishing sight.

Stephanotis (continued)

Propagation is from cuttings throughout the year; these can be rooted only in a temperature and bottom heat of 25–30°C (77–86°F). The cuttings are taken from the previous year's wood; they will root in 4–6 weeks. Seed is developed fairly freely; it is sown in warm conditions, but this method is rarely used, since plants grown this way flower much later and much less profusely than those propagated from cuttings.

The flowering season lasts from May to October, the dormant season from October to January.

☼ A well-lit, airy situation, but out of the sun

🌡 Warm (16–20°C (61–68°F) at night); minimum temperature in winter 12°C (54°F)

💧 In summer water frequently; in winter give less water

〰 Moderate humidity

🪴 Normal potting compost with the addition of leaf-mould and some loam

Strelitzia

Bird of paradise flower

Although these magnificent flowers are now used more and more frequently in professional arrangements, it is by no means usual to grow *Strelitzia reginae* (illustrated) as a house plant. Nevertheless, it is not impossible, especially if you have a well-lit, cool hall where it can spend the winter. Use good-sized tubs filled with a very nutritious, loamy mixture. Re-pot in spring or in summer, taking great care not to damage the fleshy roots. Propagation is from seed; the plants will take 4 years to flower.

☼ Keep in a well-lit, sunny spot; in summer screen against very bright sun

🌡 Moderate (12–18°C (54–64°F) at night); provide fresh air in summer as soon as the temperature rises above 21°C (70°F). In winter 10°C (50°F)

💧 Water freely in spring and summer; keep dry in winter

〰 Moderate humidity

🪴 Somewhat loamy potting mixture

Streptocarpus

Cape primrose

This flower is grown for the magnificent flowers it may produce in large numbers and for a prolonged period.

I say 'may', for the flowering depends on correct treatment and, as is the case with the African violet (*Saintpaulia*), which is grown in very similar conditions, the remarkable thing is that some people manage to grow these plants (usually *Streptocarpus* hybrids—see photographs) like weeds, while others can barely keep them in good condition for a month.

If you study the immense, hairy leaves, you will quickly realise that these plants enjoy humid air. They should therefore never be placed above a source of heat and are best grown in wide, shallow dishes. The air should be lightly mist-sprayed as often as possible, but never to the extent that the foliage retains drops of water. An east-facing window is ideal for these (and many other) plants, for they do not tolerate the bright noonday sun.

Streptocarpus is usually at its best in the second year, when it may produce many hundreds of flowers. These vary in colour from white via pink and red to reddish-purple and purple. There is also a pure blue form. The seed capsules are coiled.

In the flowering season *Streptocarpus* must be regularly fed. The plant is very easily increased in an indoor propagator. Cut a leaf across the vein and insert both sections, cut edge down, in a mixture of sand and peat. In a little while numerous plantlets will develop along the cut, which may subsequently be potted separately. They are best kept under glass or plastic at first and then gradually accustomed to drier air.

Never subject to the sun's rays, but give plenty of light

Cold to moderate (6–13°C (43–55°F) at night); minimum day temperature in winter 10°C (50°F)

Water freely in the growing period; a little less in winter, depending on the temperature

Moderate; do not spray the foliage

Potting compost mixed with leafmould and peat

Stromanthe

From the photograph it will be apparent that the *Stromanthe* genus belongs to the family of *Marantaceae*. There are 13 different species, all originating in tropical regions of South America. *Stromanthe amabilis* (photograph) has grey-green foliage with dark green marking. In *Stromanthe sanguinea* the upper surface of the leaves is dark green with a paler central vein; the underside is brownish-purple. In all species the inflorescence rises above the foliage. The plants can be increased by division or from offshoots. Treatment is as for other *Marantaceae*, such as *Calathea* and *Maranta*.

 Diffused sunlight is acceptable; direct sunrays are not

 Warm (16–20°C (61–68°F) at night); minimum temperature in winter 15°C (59°F)

 In the growing season water freely; slightly less in the dormant period. Always use tepid soft water

Fairly high degree of humidity

Porous mixture

Syngonium

Goosefoot plant

Syngonium has a number of characteristics which distinguish it from other Arum lily plants such as *Philodendron* or *Monstera*. In the first place all *Syngonium* species contain a milky liquid and in the second place the shape of the leaves varies greatly with the stages of development.

In *Syngonium vellozianum* (photograph) the leaves are initially arrow-shaped; they then become 3-lobed and later 5-lobed. The leaf-stalks are fairly long; the bracts are pale yellow. In many cases two small ear-shaped appendages develop underneath the lower lobes. *Syngonium podophyllum* may even have 11-lobed leaves.

 Shady, but definitely not too dark

 Warm (16–20°C (61–68°F) at night); minimum temperature in winter 16°C (61°F)

 Water regularly, using tepid water; a little less in winter

 Fairly high degree of humidity preferred

 Standard to chalky potting mixture

Syngonium (continued)

The adjoining photograph shows a yellow/green marbled strain of *Syngonium podophyllum*. If variegated forms are placed in too dark a position they will revert to green. More mature plants may from April to August produce greenish, monoecious flower spikes. Roots develop from the nodes.

Propagation by eye- or tip-cuttings. If using the first method, take a section of stem with an eye; let the eye develop a little before the cutting is rooted under glass, in bottom heat. Air layering, too, presents few problems. Ensure good drainage.

☼   Shady, but definitely not too dark

🌡   Warm (16–20°C (61–68°F) at night); minimum temperature in winter 16°C (61°F)

💧   Water regularly, using tepid water; a little less in winter

💨   Fairly high degree of humidity preferred

🪣   Standard to chalky potting mixture

Tetrastigma

Chestnut vine

This evergreen fast-growing climber has composite leaves, shiny green on the upper surface, brown-haired underneath. It belongs to the Vine family and originates in Vietnam. The species illustrated is *Tetrastigma voinierianum*, the only one in cultivation.

The plant may be increased throughout the year from cuttings with an eye and a leaf. It is important not to bury the eye when the cutting is rooted; this is done under glass at a temperature of 25°C (70°F).

☼   Tolerates a reasonable amount of shade

🌡   Moderate (10–16°C (50–61°F) at night); in winter allow a dormant season at 10°C (50°F)

💧   In summer give plenty of soft water; a little less in the resting period

💨   Moderate humidity

🪣   Compost-based potting soil or standard pre-packed potting compost

Thunbergia

Black-eyed Susan

This plant is easily grown from seed sown in March and germinated in a temperature of 16–18°C (61–64°F). If *Thunbergia alata* (photograph) is grown for the garden, it should, after being pricked out and potted in May, be allowed to harden a little. It is then trained up a sunny, south-facing wall. Indoors it must be supported with wire or sticks. Feed once every week or fortnight.

Although this native of South Africa is actually an annual, it may without much difficulty be kept through the winter in a greenhouse.

- ☼ Can be grown in the garden as well as indoors, but needs a sunny situation
- 🌡 Moderate to warm (13–18°C (55–64°F) at night); keep at 8–10°C (46–50°F) in winter
- 💧 Always water freely in the growing period, less in winter
- 〰 Moderate humidity
- 🪣 Standard pre-packed potting compost

Tillandsia

To date, more than five hundred species of this terrestrial and epiphytic growing bromeliad are known. Most of them are natives of Central and South America, where they thrive in all sorts of habitats.

The species illustrated is *Tillandsia cyanea*, which has an inflorescence consisting of pink bracts and violet flowers. A very similar but differently coloured species is *Tillandsia lindenii*, in which the bracts are green/pink/lilac and the flowers purplish. *Tillandsia usneoides* (Spanish moss) loses its roots when still in the seedling stage.

- ☼ Well-lit position; diffused sunlight
- 🌡 Warm (16–20°C (61–68°F) at night); minimum temperature in winter 13°C (55°F)
- 💧 Water moderately throughout the year, but especially in winter
- 〰 High degree of humidity required; e.g. deep-plate method
- 🪣 Orchid mixture containing fern roots

Tolmiea

Mother of thousands

Tolmiea menziesii (illustrated) has long-stalked, heart-shaped and hairy leaves, growing in rosettes. Offsets are developed on the leaves; these grow into plantlets and strike root as soon as the old leaf drops. The flowers appear in 25cm (10in) racemes and are green to brown in colour.

Propagation is by division or by potting the plantlets. Always provide good drainage by putting crocks in the bottom of the pot.

From May to September give liquid fertiliser once a month.

 Put in a well-lit, preferably sunny spot

 Moderate (10–16°C (50–61°F) at night); minimum temperature in winter 5°C (41°F)

 Water regularly in the growing period, sparingly in the dormant season

Moderate humidity

Friable mixture, e.g. a proprietary potting compost mixed with leafmould

Torenia

This genus comprises fifty species, of which *Torenia fournieri* (illustrated) is by far the best known. The flowers, which from July to September appear in great profusion, grow in terminal racemes. The corolla is pale violet; the three lower leaves are blotched with deep purple and the throat has yellow marking. A strain called 'Alba' has a white corolla with purple blotches; 'Grandiflora' has exceptionally large flowers.

Propagation is from seed in March; this germinates under glass in a temperature of about 18°C (64°F), and should be covered with a thin layer of sifted compost.

 Appreciates both sun and semi-shade; in summer it may be placed in a sheltered outdoor position

 Moderate (10–16°C (50–61°F) at night

 Water moderately, but make sure the soil-ball does not dry out

 Moderate humidity

 Somewhat loamy mixture

Tradescantia

Wandering Jew

Most of the sixty species of this genus originate in South America. The photograph shows (rear) *Tradescantia albiflora*, whose creeping or pendulous stems make it suitable for use as groundcover or as a hanging plant. The species has green leaves; in the strain 'Albovittata' they are cream-striped, and 'Tricolor' has foliage striped in pink, white and green. As indicated by the specific name, all these forms have white flowers.

Tradescantia blossfeldiana (foreground) is a creeping plant which continues to grow in winter. The upper surface of the leaves is green and bare, the reverse purple and hairy. The pink flowers of this native of Argentina have a white centre. The flowering season lasts from March till July. The form 'Variegata' has cream-striped foliage.

Tradescantia crassula has erect growing stems with shiny foliage, mainly at the base of the plant, and terminal growing white flowers.

Tradescantia fluminensis is very similar to *Tradescantia albiflora*, but is distinguished by its short internodes. The leaves are blue-green, and violet on the underside. Here, too, there is a striped form, 'Variegata'.

When the plants deteriorate new specimens are easily grown from cuttings; the best time to do this is between April and September. Tip-cuttings root very readily either in water or in a sandy soil mixture at a temperature of 16°C (61°F).

Re-pot in April, and from May to September give diluted liquid fertiliser every two weeks. The variegated forms need a little more light than the all-green plants.

If you possess a heated greenhouse you will find that all *Tradescantia* forms make effective groundcover under the staging.

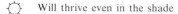

☼ Will thrive even in the shade

🌡 Moderate (10–16°C (50–61°F) at night); minimum temperature in winter 5°C (41°F)

💧 Keep the soil-ball moist; in winter the soil may dry out in between watering

☷ Fairly high degree of humidity desirable

🪣 Pre-packed potting compost

Tulipa

Tulip

For early flowering, pot the bulbs in September; otherwise in October. Use a mixture of sand and potting compost. Bury the pots in the garden—making sure the soil will not dry out—and provide adequate protection. They may also be put in a dark spot indoors, at a maximum temperature of 12°C (54°F); here, too, you should maintain adequate moisture.

When you can feel that the flower-bud has emerged from the bulb, the pots may be brought into the light. Place them in the coolest possible position at first, and occasionally spray the shoot.

☼ Semi-shade to light-shade

🌡 Moderate to warm (12–17°C (54–63°F) at night); daytime temperature about 20°C (68°F)

💧 Water normally

Moderate humidity

Mixture of pre-packed potting compost and sharp sand, with a 3–4cm (1¼–1½in) layer of drainage material at the bottom

Vallota

This beautiful bulbous plant is exceptionally well suited for indoor cultivation.

In summer the *Vallota speciosa* illustrated produces fine orange-red flowers with a diameter of about 8cm (3in).

In spring the bulbs are potted in a nutritious, friable mixture; the neck of the bulb should remain exposed. The first leaves will appear within a short time, followed by the flower-stalk. Faded flowers should be removed and the flower-stalk cut off when it has turned yellow. Propagation is from offsets which may flower in the third year.

☼ Always place in good light, but out of the sun

🌡 Moderate (10–16°C (50–61°F) at night); keep in a cool place in winter

💧 Sparingly in spring, increasing gradually; freely in summer

Moderate humidity

Friable, slightly acid mixture

Vriesea

These bromeliads are either epiphytes or terrestrial-growing. Most of the nearly two hundred species known were discovered in Mexico, the Caribbean and the northern part of South America. As a rule the evergreen leaves are shiny, with an unincised edge. The funnel-shaped rosettes may serve as water reservoirs; sometimes a complete biological balance is achieved in this micro-climate, as it might in a pond.

The upper photograph shows *Vriesea × peolmannii*, a cross between *Vriesea × gloriosa* and *Vriesea × vangeertii*; it has shiny green foliage and a brownish-red flower spike. In the lower photograph you see the well-known species *Vriesea splendens*, which has curved green leaves with brown cross-banding, and a long, flat, bright red spike from which yellow flowers appear. The pale yellow-green leaf-rosette of *Vriesea fenestralis* has dark-green, longitudinal stripes. The leaf-tips and the bracts of the inflorescence are reddish-brown; the flowers are yellow and appear at night. This is exceptional, for as a rule yellow-flowering *Vriesea* plants bloom in the daytime and white forms at night. *Vriesea hieroglyphica* originates in Brazil and is very popular because of the interesting deep purple marking, resembling hieroglyphs, on a yellow-green background. The leaf-rosette may grow to as much as a metre (40in). Flowering occurs in spring; the bracts are red with yellow margins; the flowers are yellow.

Vriesea plants may be grown from seed, but in that case it may take 10–15 years before they flower. It is simpler to pot the newly formed rooted offset rosettes; these may be removed from the mother plant when they have reached 10–15cm (4–6in). Pot them separately and keep them in a heated greenhouse. They may flower in 2–3 years.

☼ Requires moderate daylight

🌡 Warm (16–20°C (61–68°F) at night); a few degrees cooler in winter

💧 Water regularly, using tepid, soft water, which may be poured into the funnel

🖌 When kept in the living-room the plant should frequently be sprayed; *Vriesea* enjoys humid air

🪣 Bromeliad soil with sphagnum

Washingtonia

The photograph shows *Washingtonia filifera* which may be given an even cooler situation than *Washingtonia robusta*. Both species are natives of California. They may be grown from fresh seed, which must first be soaked for 2 days in a temperature of 30°C (86°F). They are then sown in a sandy mixture, under glass and at a bottom temperature of 25–30°C (77–86°F). Germination may take anything from 2 weeks to as much as 3 years. The seedlings must be treated with care. They are first pricked out in a mixture of leafmould and moorland soil. More mature plants are given a mixture of 3 parts rotted clay-based turves, 2 parts manure, 2 parts leafmould and 1 part sand.

☼ Good light preferred, but not in the sun. A degree of shade is tolerated

🌡 Moderate (10–16°C (50–61°F) at night); minimum temperature in winter 4°C (39°F)

💧 Water regularly; plunge occasionally

💨 Palms like a fairly humid atmosphere. Spray very frequently

🪴 A loamy mixture, rich in humus

Yucca

Spanish bayonet

The *Yucca*, formerly almost unknown, has in recent years become unbelievably popular, even though it is well known that in the living-room it will almost certainly die within a few years, and even though the leaves are so sharp that it has cost many a child an eye. It is very difficult to keep a *Yucca* in good condition. It will thrive only if given a very well-lit sunny position, preferably out of doors in summer; it should be kept fairly cool in winter.

The best known species, *Yucca aloifolia*, is shown in both photographs, in the correct indoor and outdoor positions. The stiff, sharply pointed leaves grow in rosettes. A particularly fine specimen is illustrated on p. 2. Of the other species, *Yucca gloriosa* is illustrated on p. 14.

Species with blunt leaves have come on the market in the last few years; time will tell how satisfactory they prove to be.

An attack by pests indicates incorrect conditions. Re-pot in the spring of every second year; provide drainage to prevent drowning.

Yucca (continued)

The best soil mixture consists of loam, sand, rotted cow manure and ordinary potting compost. Make sure that heavy plants do not overbalance. The most expensive plant displays consist of several trunks combined in a container in such a way that they form an attractive whole. To my mind they are purely a status symbol—for the same price you could buy a colour television. However, opinions differ and may in any case depend on wealth!

 In summer a warm, sunny spot out of doors. In winter a well-lit position indoors

 Moderate (10–16°C (50–61°F) at night); in winter it must be kept cool at 6°C (43°F)

 Water regularly in summer, but provide good drainage

 Stands up well to dry living-room atmosphere

 Somewhat loamy, porous mixture

Zantedeschia

Arum lily

Zantedeschia aethiopica (photograph), a native of South Africa, is the species best suited for indoor cultivation. Some forms can be grown in the garden as well. *Zantedeschia aethiopica* flowers from March to June. After flowering, put it in good light until August and cease watering. The plant may then be increased by division: the little plantlets are removed from the mother plant and potted separately. In the growing and flowering seasons water plentifully, using soft water. Feed every week.

Propagation can also be by division of the rootstock.

 Well-lit, sunny position on the balcony or in the garden. Bring indoors in late September

 Moderate (10–16°C (50–61°F) at night); keep at 8–10°C (46–50°F) in winter

 Give plenty of soft water in summer; provide good drainage

 Requires a fairly humid atmosphere indoors

 Calcareous potting mixture, rich in humus

Zebrina

This plant is related to the better known *Tradescantia*. It is easily grown, especially in plant troughs, and is regularly used as groundcover in greenhouses. In pots on the windowsill it may be rather more difficult to cultivate, especially where there is hot air rising from a central heating radiator.

The best known species is *Zebrina pendula*, which has two wide silvery stripes on the foliage. In the 'Quadricolor' strain (illustrated) red and pink shades occur as well. The coloration depends largely on the light available.

Propagation is from cuttings.

☀ Light to half-shade

🌡 Warm (16–20°C (61–68°F) at night); in winter preferably not below 12°C (54°F)

💧 Water regularly with lime-free water; in winter keep slightly less moist

💨 Fairly high degree of humidity

🪴 Lighten pre-packed potting compost by the addition of sand

Zygocactus

Christmas cactus

The Christmas cactus is an easy and rewarding jointed cactus, which should not be confused with the Easter cactus (see *Rhipsalidopsis*). In this plant the tubular flowers consist of corollae at two levels; as a rule they are violet, sometimes red. After flowering the plant should be allowed to rest by witholding water, but the joints must not shrivel up. In early June it is advisable to put it in a shady spot in the garden, but beware of slugs. Feed until the beginning of August. Bring indoors at the end of September and keep fairly dry until the flowerbuds appear. Propagation is from cuttings.

The forms in cultivation are mainly hybrids.

☀ Slightly diffused sunlight will do no harm; a half-shady position is preferable

🌡 Water normally, except in the dormant season

💧 Moderate (10–16°C (50–61°F) at night); after September keep dry and cool until the flowerbuds appear

💨 Humid air and regular spraying are much appreciated

🪴 Leafmould mixed with some clay and sand

Appendix

The following surveys may help you in building up plant displays. The most important house plants described in this book have been tabled according to their ideal requirements. In most cases this does not mean that they would die in other conditions. For more detailed information consult the plant descriptions.

Full sun

These are all plants which can live all day near an unscreened, south-facing window. The terms 'cool', 'moderate' and 'warm' refer to night temperatures in summer. Most plants prefer cooler conditions in winter.

Cool: *temperature at night 5–10°C (41–50°F)*

Acacia	Euonymus	Narcissus	Solanum
Cytisus	Lachenalia	Oxalis	
Dionaea	Lilium	Pittosporum	
Erica	Myrtus	Sempervivum	

Moderate: *temperature at night 10–16°C (50–61°F)*

Abutilon	Cuphea	Lithops	Senecio succulenten
Agapanthus	Echeveria	Pachyphytum	Sparmannia
Ageratum	Echinocereus	× Pachyveria	Strelitzia
Aloe	Felicia	Passiflora	Tolmiea
Aporocactus	Hamatocactus	Plumbago	Thunbergia
Beloperone	Iresine	Punica	Yucca
Chamaerops	Lantana	Rosa	Zantedeschia
Citrus	Laurus	Sedum	

Warm: *temperature at night 16–20°C (61–68°F)*

Allamanda	Coleus	Hibiscus	Notocactus
Ananas	Cotyledon	Homalocladium	Opuntia
Bougainvillea	Echinocactus	Ipomoea	Pachypodium
Canna	Echinopsis	Lampranthus	Parodia
Cephalocereus	Espostoa	Lobivia	Pseudomammillaria
Cereus	Euphorbia milii	Mammillaria	Rebutia
Cleistocactus	Gasteria	Neoporteria	Stapelia
Codiaeum	Haemanthus	Nerium	Stenotaphrum

Shady position

The plants in this category do not tolerate full sun. If placed near a
south-facing window they must be screened from 10 am to 4 pm. They
can live all day near an unscreened east- or west-facing window. The
plants marked with an asterisk will stand even deep shade. The absolute
minimum of light required is 1000–1500 lux (see p. 7).

Cool: *temperature at night 5–10°C (41–50°F)*

Aucuba*	Crocus	Hedera*	Rochea
Azalea	Cyclamen	Lilium	Rhoicissus*
Calceolaria	× Fatshedera*	Myrtus	Senecio cruentus
Camellia	Fatsia*	Phyllitis*	Skimmia
Campanula	Hebe	Primula	Streptocarpus

Moderate: *temperature at night 10–16°C (50–61°F)*

Ampleopsis	Chrysanthemum	Hydrangea	Pteris*
Araucaria	Cissus*	Impatiens	Rhoeo
Ardisia	Clerodendrum	Jasminum	Saxifraga
Asparagus*	Cleyerea	Liriope	Schefflera*
Aspidistra*	Clivia	Lycaste	Selaginella*
Asplenium*	Cyperus	Microlepia*	Soleirolia
Begonia	Duchesnea	Nephrolepis	Tetrastigma*
Billbergia	Epiphyllum	Nertera	Torenia
Browallia	Fuchsia	Odontoglossum	Tradescantia, groen*
Capsicum	Grevillea	Ophiopogon*	Tulipa
Carex	Gymnocalycium	Pellaea*	Vallota
Catharanthus	Habranthus	Phoenix	Washingtonia
Ceropegia	Hippeastrum	Pilea	Zygocactus
Chamaedorea	Howeia*	Plectranthus	

Warm: *temperature at night 16–20°C (61–68°F)*

Achimenes	Ctenanthe	Medinilla	Rhaphidophora*
Adiantum*	Cyrtomium*	Microcoelum	Rechsteineria
Aechmea	Didymochlaena*	Mimosa	Rhipsalidopsis
Aeschynanthus	Dieffenbachia	Monstera*	Saintpaulia
Aglaonema	Dipladenia	Neoregelia	Sansevieria*
Alocasia	Dipteracanthus	Nidularium	Scindapsus
Anthurium	Dizygotheca	Oplismenus	Scirpus
Aphelandra	Dracaena	Pachystachys	Siderasis*
Begonia	Episcia	Pandanus	Sinningia
Bertolonia*	Ficus*	Pavonia	Smithiantha
Blechnum*	Fittonia	Pellionia	Sonerila
Caladium	Gardenia	Peperomia	Spathiphyllum
Calathea*	Guzmania	Pereskia	Stenandrium
Chlorophytum*	Gynura	Philodendron	Stephanotis
Codiaeum	Hemigraphis*	Phlebodium	Stromanthe
Coelogyne	Hoya	Pilea	Syngonium*
Columnea	Hypocyrta	Piper	Tillandsia
Cordyline	Hypoestes	Pisonia	Vriesea
Crassula	Ixora	Polyscias	Zebrina
Crossandra	Jacaranda	Polystichum	
Cryptanthus	Maranta	Pseuderanthemum	

Humidity

In centrally heated homes the plants listed under 'high' can be grown successfully only with the aid of an evaporator or the 'deep plate' method. Regular spraying is less effective.

High

Acalypha	Haemanthus	Odontoglossum	
Adiantum	Hoya	Pellionia	Selaginella
Allamanda	Hypocyrta	Peperomia	Siderasis
Bertolonia	Hypoestes	Phlebodium	Smithiantha
Calathea	Ixora	Phyllitis	Soleirolia
Coelogyne	Jacaranda	Piper	Spathiphyllum
Columnea	Lycaste	Polyscias	Stenandrium
Cordyline	Maranta	Polystichum	Stromanthe
Cryptanthus	Medinilla	Pseuderanthemum	Tillandsia
Cyrtomium	Microlepia	Pteris	Tradescantia
Dionaea	Neoregelia	Rechsteineria	Vriesea
Dipladenia	Nephrolepis	Saintpaulia	Washingtonia
Fittonia	Nertera	Scindapsus	Zantedeschia
Fuchsia	Nidularium	Scirpus	Zebrina

Moderate

Abutilon	Cytisus	Laurus	Primula
Aechmea	Dipteracanthus	Lilium	Punica
Ageratum	Dizygotheca	Liriope	Rhipsalidopsis
Aglaonema	Dracaena	Microcoelum	Rhoeo
Anthurium	Duchesnea	Mimosa	Rhoicissus
Araucaria	Epiphyllum	Monstera	Rochea
Asparagus	Euphorbia pulcherrima	Myrtus	Saxifraga
Asplenium	Exacum	Narcissus	Schefflera
Azalea	× Fatshedera	Neoporteria	Senecio
Beloperone	Fatsia	Ophiopogon	Setcreasea
Bougainvillea	Gardenia	Oplismenus	Sinningia
Browallia	Grevillea	Oxalis	Skimmia
Brunfelsia	Gynura	Pachystachys	Solanum
Caladium	Haemanthus	Pandanus	Stenotaphrum
Calceolaria	Hibiscus	Paphiopedilum	Stephanotis
Camellia	Hippeastrum	Passiflora	Strelitzia
Canna	Homocladium	Pavonia	Streptocarpus
Carex	Howeia	Pellaea	Syngonium
Catharanthus	Hyacinthus	Pereskia	Tetrastigma
Chamaedorea	Hydrangea	Persea	Thunbergia
Cissus	Impatiens	Philodendron	Tolmiea
Citrus	Ipomoea	Phoenix	Torenia
Cleyera	Iresine	Pilea	Tulipa
Codiaeum	Jacobinia	Pisonia	Vallota
Coleus	Lachenalia	Pittosporum	
Cuphea	Lantana	Plumbago	

Low

Aeonium	Cotyledon	Gasteria	Pachypodium
Agave	Crassula	Gymnocalycium	Parodia
Aloe	Echeveria	Hamatocactus	Platycerium
Ampelopsis	Echinocactus	Lampranthus	Pseudomammillaria
Aporocactus	Echinopsis	Lithops	Raphidophora
Astrophytum	Espostoa	Lobivia	Sedum
Cereus	Euphorbia milii	Nerium	Sempervivum
Ceropegia	Euphorbia succulenten	Opuntia	Stapelia
Clivia	Faucaria	Pachyphytum	Yucca

187

Soil

All plants do best in the type of soil most closely resembling that in their native habitat. The species listed below have been roughly divided according to their soil requirements: calcareous, normal and acid. For suitable mixtures see the introduction. Plants with very special requirements, such as, for instance, orchids, bromeliads, cacti, *Anthurium*, etc., have not been listed.

For further details see the plant descriptions.

Calcareous

Abutilon	Faucaria	Mimosa	Sempervivum
Agave	Felicia	Nerium	Senecio
Asparagus	Ficus	Oxalis	Solanum
Capsicum	Gasteria	Passiflora	Stenotaphrum
Catharanthus	Grevillea	Pittosporum	Strelitzia
Cissus	Hedera	Plumbago	Torenia
Clerodendrum	Homocladium	Polyscias	Washingtonia
Crocus	Howeia	Rhoicissus	Yucca
Cyclamen	Jacobinia	Rochea	Zantedeschia
Cyperus	Jasminum	Sansevieria	
Cytisus	Lachenalia	Schefflera	
Euphorbia	Lithops	Scirpus	

Normal

Ageratum	Exacum	Pandanus	Scindapsus
Ananas	Gynura	Philodendron	Smithiantha
Billbergia	Hebe	Phlebodium	Stenandrium
Bougainvillea	Impatiens	Phoenix	Stephanotis
Calceolaria	Ipomoea	Pilea	Streptocarpus
Canna	Laurus	Plectranthus	Syngonium
Chlorophytum	Liriope	Polystichum	Tetrastigma
Cleyera	Maranta	Pseuderanthemum	Thunbergia
Coleus	Microcoelum	Rhaphidophora	Tolmiea
Cordyline	Monstera	Rhipsalidopsis	Tradescantia
Dizygotheca	Narcissus	Rhoeo	Zebrina
Duchesnea	Pachystachys	Rosa	

Acid

Achimenes	Cotyledon	Hypocyrta	Piper
Adiantum	Ctenanthe	Hypoestes	Saintpaulia
Araucaria	Dionaea	Jacaranda	Skimmia
Azalea	Erica	Microlepia	Sonerila
Callistemon	Guzmania	Notocactus	Spathiphyllum
Camellia	Hoya	Pellaea	

Index

Photograph Credits

All the photographs in this book were taken
by Bob Herwig, with the exception of:

   Aporocactus flagelliformis—J. van Dommelen
   Felicia amelloides—W. Stehling
   Selenicereus grandiflorus—J. van Dommelen

The author would like to acknowledge the help
in the preparation of this book of Ines Girisch,
Esther van Duijvendijk and the following
organizations:

AMEV, Hoofdkantoor—Utrecht
Hotel Atlanta—Amsterdam
N.V. Handelskwekerij Gebr.
   Barendsen—Aalsmeer
The Botany departments of the State
   University of Leiden, the State University of
   Utrecht and the Free University of
   Amsterdam
Bruinsma's Tuin-Dorado—Aalsmeer
Cactuskwekerij C.V. Bulthuis en Co.—Cothen
Floreat! Hydrokultuur—Velp

The classification system used in this book
follows Zander, *Handwörterbuch der
Pflanzennamen*, Stuttgart, 1972

Franzen, Hey & Veltman/BBDO—Amsterdam
Hoek's broeiproevenbedridjf—Oude Niedorp
De heer en mevrouw Hopf—Amstelveen
Instituut voor de Veredeling van
   Tuinbouwgewassen—Wageningen
Jolina Bloemiste—Amsterdam
Jolina Twins—Amsterdam
Laboratorium voor Bloembollenonderzoek
   —Lisse
Handelskwekerij Fa. A. Maarse Kzn.
   —Rijsenhout
Gebr. K. & C. van der Meer—Aalsmeer
Proefstation voor de Bloemisterij—Aalsmeer
Trend Communications—Amsterdam
Bloemist R. Vogels—Wateringen